P9-DIY-967

A Saddlebag Guide for Dudes, Tenderfeet, and Cowpunchers Everywhere

THE COWBOY LIFE

·

MICHELE MORRIS

ILLUSTRATIONS BY LARRY BUTE

A Fireside Book ★ Published by Simon & Schuster
New York London Toronto Sydney Tokyo Singapore

A Saddlebag Guide for Dudes, Tenderfeet, and Cowpunchers Everywhere
A Saddlebag Guide for Dudes, Tenderfeet, and Cowpunchers Everywhere
A Saddlebag Guide for Dudes, Tenderfeet, and Cowpunchers Everywhere

FIRESIDE
Rockefeller Center
1230 Avenue of the Americas
New York, New York 10020

Copyright © 1993 by Michele Morris

FIRESIDE and colophon are registered trademarks
of Simon & Schuster Inc.

Designed by Bonni Leon-Berman
Manufactured in the United States of America

1 3 5 7 9 10 8 6 4 2

Library of Congress Cataloging-in-Publication Data
Morris, Michele.
The cowboy life : a saddlebag guide for dudes, tenderfeet, and
cowpunchers everywhere / Michele Morris.
p.   cm.
"A Fireside book."
1. Cowboys—West (U.S.)   2. West (U.S.)—Social life and customs.
I. Title.
F596.M685   1993   93-25257
636.2'13'0978—dc20   CIP

ISBN 0-671-86682-6

For Nick and Jack.

May you one day have

a chance to cowboy.

Acknowledgments

Here's to all the cowboys I have known and loved. Special thanks to my father, who taught me the cowboy code; my mother, who gave me the ranch heritage, my brothers, who embody the buckaroo spirit; and my husband, who always gave me a cowboy song. For their stories and insights, I owe a bucket of gratitude to Sheila Morris and Rob Gaebe; Bernadette and Bill Connor; John Mike Downey; Mary Ann and Vince Carey; Shawn Davis, and dozens of other cowpunchers. A gold buckle to buckaroo artist Larry Bute, whose contributions went far beyond the illustrations.

I tip my hat to my tenderfoot friends, especially Ronni Sandroff, Amanda Smith, Howard Friedman, my agent Joe Spieler, who spurred me on, and my editor Gary Luke, who rode herd on the project.

With gratitude to the efforts of Erin Murray, Walt Hinick, Hal Stearns, William Campbell, the staffs of the Butte Public Library, the Montana Historical Society, the Wyoming State Museum, the Arizona State Historical Society, the Buffalo Bill Historical Center, the National Cowboy Hall of Fame, the Cowgirl Hall of Fame, the Professional Rodeo Cowboys Association, and the Women's Professional Cowboy Association.

★ Where the road ends and the trail begins. (*Stephen Collector*) ★

CONTENTS

THE COWBOY HERO

MY GRANDFATHER WAS a cowboy. He started out as a sheep rancher, but too many years of walking behind wool made him long for better vistas. Determined to raise cattle, he sold his sheep, bought himself a herd, and rode horseback.

Bopa Joe's luck was better than most cowboys. Many working hands dream of having their own ranch someday, but spend their days riding for another man's brand. Bopa's brand, the Three-handled Frying Pan, was his own. He won it through long Montana days, interrupted nights, an iron fist, and a tight purse. He could stand on the bank of the Jefferson River and look south toward the Tobacco Root Mountains and know that his cattle grazed all the way to the timberline without crossing a border fence.

It wasn't easy then to live the cowboy life. It's even harder now. The cowboy is in danger of being squeezed right off the land he loves. The price of good ranch land is soaring as rich cityfolk and movie stars pay inflated prices for scenery. Most cowboys work on land they can never hope to own. Hard work and good luck aren't enough to guarantee the down payment on a family ranch when you're bidding against baseball players and beer companies.

But despite all this, cowboy culture is alive and kicking. To be a cowboy is a calling, and it has a special unbroken tie to the past. He still can rope steers, break horses, and ride like the wind. The ranch has become the last best place and rodeo has become a growing spectator sport. The cowboy mystique (with special thanks to Hollywood) is just too strong to disappear. He represents an island of strength and sanity in a complicated world. Living the cowboy life is the dream that keeps many a rodeo cowboy going down the road, brings many a rancher's son home from the big city, and calls many a tenderfoot out west.

Little wonder that the cowboy life is being portrayed in poetry, celebrated in song, and emulated on weekends by cowboys who rope their paychecks from behind a desk. Maybe they once cowboyed before they had a family, a mortgage, an education. But the cowboy life has a hold on them. It holds them with a long, strong rope.

Here's hoping that one day you'll enjoy a sunset on horseback, a meal cooked over an open fire, and the feel of a good saddle. May you always ride a good horse.

—Michele Morris

(the Rocking Double M, my personal brand)

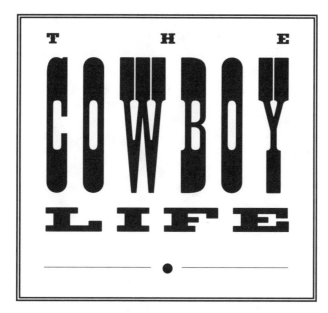

COWBOYS TODAY

THE SUN COMES up over Bull Mountain just as Vince Carey rides out of cow camp, ready to round up the cattle grazing in Lockhart Meadows and bring them down from the mountains. He spends the day making a circle of the pastureland, trailing any cattle he finds back to camp. Mounted on his big sorrel horse, Red, with his son John on one side and his dog Pigger on the

★ *(Library of Congress)* ★

other, Carey later trails the cattle down the two-lane highway that snakes through Montana's North Boulder Valley. The entire journey will take two weeks, two of the best weeks of the year for Carey. He and his uncle and cousins (who own the neighboring ranch) ride good horses all day and camp out all night. There's a camaraderie around the campfire as they drink coffee and talk of women and horses and old cowpunchers.

There's only one place where a cowboy can follow his way of life: on a ranch. If he's been blessed, he's the rancher's son and the ranch is paid for. If he's not, he'll be happy if the horses are fast, the country is open, and the chuck is great.

It's impossible to tell from looking at Carey as he rides into the daylight that he is head of a prosperous ranching family. Dressed in faded Wrangler jeans, an old canvas jacket, and a well-seasoned cowboy hat, Carey looks like any other cowboy, but he's actually a vanishing breed: a third-generation rancher. He and his wife, the daughter and granddaughter of ranchers, live in a seventy-year-old red clapboard house with a wide shady porch in front and a pasture full of cattle in back. The ranch is big enough to support the extended family, pay the bills, and put something in the bank, but it's small enough that all but one of the cowboys riding for the 70 brand are family members.

"I've got the best life in the world," says Carey, who grew up in the valley and has no plans ever to leave. His dream is to pass the ranch on to his son, who rides with him after school and on weekends. In the meantime, Carey is teaching his son cowboy values like responsibility ("Don't forget to close the gate!") and honesty ("Keep your word good!").

Ranch owners used to hire cowboys to tend the cattle, but today they more typically do it themselves. That's just one of the reasons that it's hard for a cowboy to find a good job these days. When he does, more often than not it's for $700 to $1,200 a month. That usually includes room and board, horse feed, sometimes gas, maybe a side of beef. Not much stuffing when you consider that a good hat costs $200; a custom saddle, two months pay; custom boots, maybe a week's pay.

Such is the life of the ranch cowboy, the mythic American hero. He takes pride in his horsemanship and roping. He's not locked up in an office. His commute is a walk across the barnyard to the horse corral. He's on better terms with Mother Nature than human nature. "I see the moose and elk wander around," says one Wyoming cowboy. "I see eagles, hawks, deer, and coyotes."

When you ask a cowboy what he does for a living, he answers, "I cowboy." Out west, *cowboy* is a verb as much as a noun. Buzz Kirkpatrick is a cowboy who ranches in Montana's Big Hole Valley. "Sometimes I think that it's a disease," he says. "It's a way of life. It's all I've ever done—and all I ever want to do."

A cowboy's work is determined by the seasons, the weather. His job, after all, is taking care of the cattle. In order to do that, he has to make sure that the fences will hold up, that the calves are branded and vaccinated, that the cattle are moved to and from summer pasture. When the cattle are grazing in the hills, he's helping put up hay for the long winter.

Cowboy Wisdom

Never walk when you can ride. And never stand when you can sit.

A man is not born a cowboy. He becomes one.

Behind every successful rancher is a wife who works in town.

"Cowboying is a rough way of life," says Kirkpatrick. I've been kicked by horses, run over by bad cows." Despite the prevalence of four-wheeled vehicles and high-priced machinery, the cowboy will never become extinct. "They just ain't come up with anything that will take as much abuse as a cowboy," replies one cowboy.

Cowboy Wisdom

A cowboy is a man with guts

and a horse.

★ Bringing home the herd. (*Stephen Collector*) ★

LIKES AND DISLIKES

While cowboys can be gentlemen, they are not boy scouts. Gene Autry used to promote the Ten Cowboy Commandments, which make cowboys sound like choirboys. (Number ten was "He must be a patriot.") Roy Rogers never drank, smoked, spit, shot pool, or kissed his girl, but these are all habits in which cowboys indulge seriously. Here's a list of the cowboy's likes and dislikes:

Cowboys like:

- women
- beer
- pickup trucks
- ponies that don't quit
- Wrangler jeans
- boots that fit
- guitars
- dancing
- living under a hat
- campfires
- rodeos
- beef
- poker
- poetry
- pitching horseshoes
- being their own boss
- wide open spaces
- springtime

Cowboys dislike:

- bosses
- driving
- officers of the law
- neckties
- people messing with their hats
- big cities
- rap music
- urban cowboys
- paperwork
- Levi 501s
- neatly trimmed beards
- office jobs
- sheep
- vegetarians
- answering letters
- golf
- boating
- wimps

THE COWBOY CODE

A cowboy

- keeps his word.
- doesn't mess with another man's horse.
- doesn't cut in front of another rider on a trail, or crowd him from behind.
- doesn't make somebody else do *all* the work.
- doesn't borrow a horse without first asking.
- doesn't wave when he meets another rider on a trail. (It might scare the horses.)
- never talks down to anyone. (If one cowboy dismounts, the other one does too.)
- always closes gates behind him.
- removes his spurs before entering the house or getting into his pick-up truck.
- doesn't leave spur marks on a horse's flesh.
- doesn't cuss another man's dog.
- knows that a clean saddle blanket is more important than clean sheets.
- never knocks down another man's fence.
- never steals another man's wife.
- puts away his horse before he puts away his dinner.
- picks the easiest route when climbing mountains on horseback.
- never rides a horse along a hard surface road, but to the side where the ground is soft.
- never gives a horse too much work.
- never jumps his horse into a run if he has a long way to travel.
- knows which way the wind is blowing and never kicks dirt in another man's plate.
- never makes anyone wait for him.
- takes his assigned place on a roundup and ends the day in the same place, between the same two riders—whether they've crossed mountains, rivers, or prairies.

★ These cowboys go by the book: chinks, spurs, and chew. (*James Fain*) ★

BIRTH OF THE COWBOY

★ Early cowboys owned little more than the clothes on their backs. (*Montana Historical Society*) ★

MOST PEOPLE THINK of the cowboy as American as apple pie, but he actually has his roots south of the Rio Grande in Mexico. The first North American cowboys were sixteenth-century Mexican horsemen called *vaqueros*, meaning those who work with cows. When Cortes imported Andalusian cattle into Mexico, he needed men to tend the herds. After the war, he branded many Indian captives on the cheek with the letter *G* for *guerra*, meaning war. Many of these Indians were sold to the first Mexican ranchers to work cattle. Ironically, cowboys wore a brand before cattle did.

Spanish missionaries drove cattle into California in 1769, long before there was any serious cattle ranching in Texas. In fact, they weren't very interested in the land north of the Rio Grande. A soldier sent to explore came back with a grim report: "No gold. Nothing but buffalo and sky."

The Mexican clergy found greener pastures in California, where they started dozens of large mission ranches. While the friars tended their flocks, someone had to tend the herds. That job fell to the Indians, who were taught to ride by friars in long brown robes.

By the time of the Mexican revolt against Spain in 1821, ranching was big business in California. The mission fathers were replaced by private owners, who were given huge land grants. Sailing ships from Boston, their holds filled with fancy clothing and furniture,

Cowboy Wisdom

A cowboy who says he's never been throwed ain't telling the entire truth.

A man on foot is not man at all.

★

would stop along the California coastline to do some trading. They hoped to return home with cowhides and tallow, the fat used to make candles and soap. The *rancheros'* taste was so expensive (they were partial to ornate beds and fine linens) that they would have to slaughter thousands of cattle to pay their bills. Trading was so brisk that cowhides were known to sailors as "California bank notes."

Both cattle and horses were plentiful, and *vaqueros* never walked if they could ride. And when they did, they rode only stallions. "It was not considered a proper or becoming thing for a lady or gentleman to ride a mare," wrote one observer. "It would, in fact, have been regarded as humiliating."

Their skill with a lariat was also

★ An early *vaquero* rode tall and saw far.
(*Arizona Historical Society/Tucson*) ★

unmatched. "I have seen some very good riders in Mexico, but these Californians are much better," wrote one Easterner who visited California in 1849. "They will throw the lasso better with their feet than Mexicans can with the hand."

The California cattle business changed when gold was discovered. Suddenly there was a ready market for beef. One Henry Miller saw gold in ranching rather than mining. He offered wages to the *vaqueros,* who were used to working for room and board. Soon men looking for work headed for Miller's place. They learned the *vaquero* skills and then moved on, to try their luck in Nevada, Oregon, Idaho, and Utah. As they became more Americanized, the Spanish was anglicized, turning "*vaquero*" into "buckaroo."

Meanwhile, on the other side of the Rocky Mountains,

THE TRAIL DRIVE

POINT RIDER

POINT RIDER

SWING RIDER

FLANK RIDER

SWING RIDER

FLANK RIDER

DRAG RIDERS

★ SPANISH ROOTS ★

It helps to speak a little Spanish around the corral. The *vaqueros* gave the cowboys most of their words for gear, cattle, and horses. But the cowboy promptly said the words his own way. Here's a sampler:

Bosal (muzzle)	Bosal	Jaquima (a halter)	Hackamore
Bronco (rough or rude)	Bronc	Juzgado (jail)	Hoosegow
Caballo (horse)	Cayuse	Lazo (noose)	Lasso
Chaparejos (leg protectors)	Chaps	Mecate (horsehair reins)	McCarty
Chincaderas (chopped off)	Chinks	Mesteño (a stray)	Mustang
Cincha (girth)	Cinch	Rancho (a soldier's mess)	Ranch
Cocinero (cook)	Cookie	Reata (rope)	Lariat
Corral (farmyard)	Corral	Rodear (to round up)	Rodeo
Dar la vuelta (give a turn)	Dally	Tapaderos (covers)	Taps
Fiador (a cord on a bridle)	Theodore	Vaquero (cow-man)	Buckaroo
Honda (the eye of a rope)	Honda		

★ After the rain in the rope corral. (*Montana Historical Society*) ★

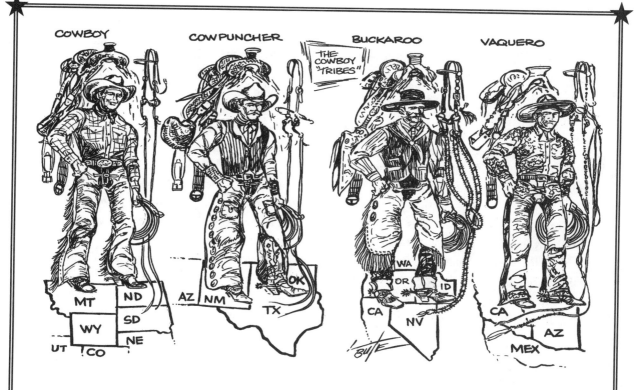

COWBOY COWPUNCHER BUCKAROO VAQUERO

THE COWBOY "TRIBES"

cattle ranches were developing in Texas. The word *cowboy* was a slur before the Civil War. In the 1830s it was applied to gangs of Anglos who would slip across the border into Mexico and steal cattle by the light of the moon. They would stampede a large herd and then run as many cat-

★

Cowboy Wisdom

A man who's honest with himself

will be honest with others.

★

tle as possible across the Rio Grande.

After the Texas Revolution and the bloody Alamo, Texans developed a prejudice toward all things Mexican. If the *vaqueros* dallied their ropes, the Texans would tie hard and fast. If the *vaqueros* used a long rope, the Texans would opt for short. The single-cinch California saddle was replaced by a double-rigged Texas saddle. Out went the spade and ring bit and in came the grazing bit.

In *Trails Plowed Under*, Charles M. Russell had this to say about the cowboy: "The cowpuncher east of the Rockies originated in Texas and ranged north to the Big Bow. He wasn't so much for pretty; his saddle was low horn, rimfire, or double-cinch. Their rope was seldom over forty feet, for being a great deal in a brush country, they were forced to swing a small loop. These men generally tied, instead of taking their dallie-welts, or wrapping their rope around the saddle horn. Their chaparejos were made of heavy bullhide, to protect the leg from brush an' thorns, with hog-snout tapaderos."

It was after the Civil War that the cowboy was rehabilitated and came into his golden years. Weary soldiers and freed slaves were being reborn as cowboys. The Texas cowboys, often black or Hispanic, spread far and wide after the Civil War, driving Texas longhorns north to the railroads in Kansas. Many kept on going, settling in New Mexico, Oklahoma, Colorado, Wyoming, Montana, and Canada.

LIFE ON THE OPEN RANGE

EARLY COWBOYS WERE drifters, with too much tumbleweed in their blood to settle down. They often owned nothing more than the clothes on their backs and the boots on their feet; making do was a way of life. In the Southwest they slept in "Tucson beds," made by lying on your back and covering yourself with your front. If they weren't sleeping on the ground, cowboys slept on feedbag mattresses stuffed with "Montana feathers," or straw.

"Living that kind of life they were bound to be wild and brave," wrote cowboy E. C. "Teddy Blue" Abbot in his autobiographical *We Pointed Them North*. "In fact there was only two things the old-time cowpuncher was afraid of, a decent woman and being set afoot."

★ In the early days, a bed was where you found it. (*Montana Historical Society*) ★

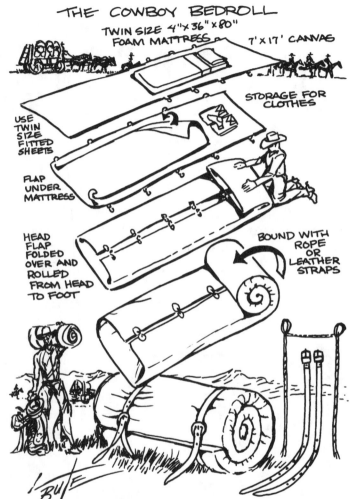

THE COWBOY BEDROLL

TWIN SIZE 4"x 36"x 80" FOAM MATTRESS

7' x 17' CANVAS

USE TWIN SIZE FITTED SHEETS

FLAP UNDER MATTRESS

STORAGE FOR CLOTHES

HEAD FLAP FOLDED OVER AND ROLLED FROM HEAD TO FOOT

BOUND WITH ROPE OR LEATHER STRAPS

The cowboys' job was to keep an eye on the cattle, the sky, and the trail. If they were lucky, they owned a saddle; if they didn't they used one of the ranch's old rigs. Because horses tired, or hurt a foot, or were good for different jobs, ranches supported *remudas,* strings of horses. Each cowboy's string might include a dozen or more horses; this way he would always have a fresh mount. Since a cowboy never knew what kind of a horse he would be given (horses were assigned on the basis of seniority), he was expected to be able to ride any mount. Many cow horses were wild horses that were domesticated by unsuspecting cowboys.

All the cattle were out west but the buyers were back east. The old law of supply and demand meant that a cow worth $5 to $10 in Texas, would fetch $20 to $40 up north. It was up to the cowboys to get the cattle to market, which meant driving them to the closest railroad station, a state or two away. In the 1860s and 1870s trail herds averaged 2,500 to 3,000 cattle. The cow to cowboy ratio was about three hundred to one. In *Log of the Cowboy,* Andy Adams recounts a lesson given by trail boss Jim Flood to greenhorns over breakfast:

★ Branding on the open range. (*Montana Historical Society*) ★

★ There was an art to saddling a wild horse. (*Montana Historical Society*) ★

Boys, the secret of trailing cattle is never to let your herd know that they are under restraint. Let everything that is done be done voluntarily by the cattle. From the moment you let them off the bed ground in the morning until they are bedded at night, never let a cow take a step, except in the direction of its destination. In this manner you can loaf away the day, and cover from fifteen to twenty miles, and the herd in the meantime will enjoy all the freedom of the open range.

A cowboy's assigned post on a drive gave him rank. The trail boss rode ahead to scout for water and grass. Cookie followed in the chuck wagon. Top hands rode "point," at the front of the herd, the post of honor. Tenderfeet rode "drag," at the back of the herd, eating dust the whole way. The rest filled in between, riding "swing" and "flank." Depending on the terrain, they covered roughly fifteen miles a day. At the end of the trail, a cowboy earned his pay—about a dollar a day— and a new nickname—cowpuncher—a name derived from the poles used to punch or prod cattle into the box cars.

It took courage, endurance, and wits to drive thousands of head of cattle to the nearest railroad. The dangers along the way included hostile Indians, raging rivers (most cowboys couldn't swim), wandering buffalo herds, dried-up water holes, cattle thieves, and stampedes. Despite the perils, the ambition of every cowboy in Texas was to go north on the legendary Chisholm Trail.

Cowboy Wisdom

It's a big mistake to drive black cattle in the dark.

Most men are like a barbed wire fence—they have their good points.

★

The wide open spaces were finally doomed by a prickly rival—barbed wire. Wooden fences were expensive. The galvanized wire fences that some farmers had started to use were no match for determined cattle and buffalo. A little nudge and the fence was history. Moreover, they were expensive. "It takes $1.74 worth of fences to keep $1.65 worth of stock from eating up $2.45 worth of crops," moaned one farmer.

Before the West was fenced, the range was considered common land. Ranchers let their cattle graze as far as their ruminant stomachs would take them. In springtime the cattle were rounded up and sorted out and the new calves were branded. Calves were roped and dragged over to a branding fire to receive their hot tattoo. Cowboys admired ropers who could keep three branding teams busy and still have time to roll a cigarette. After their work was done, cowboys often held impromptu rodeos, showing off their roping skills or trying to ride a wild horse.

Inventors like Joseph Glidden thought that they had a better idea. After seeing a fence at a county fair, Glidden, a farmer by trade, went home to tinker. Using his wife's coffee mill he came up with a twisted wire with two points. His invention won him a patent in 1874 and lost him a friend, Jacob Haish, a lumberman who also came up with a barbed wire model. By 1884 the government had granted more than 250 patents for barbed wire. (Today only one or two varieties are used.)

The wire was popular among farmers who wanted to enclose their cropland, but ranchers didn't like the idea of their precious beef on the

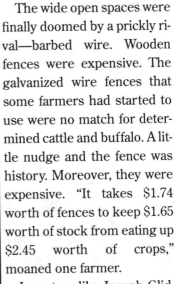

hoof being sliced into flank steak by the tiny barbs. This was the job for a true salesman, who appeared in the form of John W. Gates. Gates was having no luck selling "bob-wire" in Texas until he took a page from a flashy medicine showman: proof before purchase. Gates got permission from the town fathers in San Antonio to erect a temporary corral downtown. Then he invited local ranchers to bring their leanest, meanest longhorns to test the wire, which he claimed was "light as air, stronger than whiskey, and cheaper than dirt." The cattle were no match for the ugly little barbs. After a few thorny attempts at freedom, the cattle settled down to graze and Gates settled down to take orders.

Barbed wire spread across the open range like wildfire, closing off water holes, blocking cattle trails. When it came down to fence or be fenced, cattlemen jumped on the bandwagon. Besides protecting their turf from encroaching "nesters" (homesteaders), they soon realized, fences allowed them to keep their herds intact and improve their breeds. Riding fence became a new cowboy chore. There's something menacing about a long stretch of barbed wire fence. If you've ever cut your finger on one, you'll understand why cowboys used to call it "the devil's hat band." Fence cutters were the cause of many full-scale range wars. Even today, cutting a neighbor's fence goes against the cowboy code. Loose wire on the ground is a rider's nightmare if his horse gets entangled.

To a cattleman, cattle rustlers were the pirates of the plains. Rustlers marked unbranded calves with their own brand; changed the brands on steers and killed cattle on the open range. When the problem reached epidemic proportions, cattlemen took the law into their own hands and hired fence riders who were ordered to shoot first and ask questions later. Pink Higgins, a Matador Ranch fence rider, once came across a rustler starting to skin a cow. When Pink spied the Matador brand, he shot the thief, slit open the cow, and laid the man's body inside. Then he rode into town and nonchalantly told the sheriff that if he rode out to the Matador, he'd find a miracle of nature—a cow giving birth to a man.

Cowboy Wisdom

A horse in the corral is worth two in the brush.

Always drink upstream from the herd.

WHO WAS WHO IN THE OLD WEST

S. BURKE BURNETT was a Texas rancher who never forgot how he got his start. His brand was 6666, called the four sixes. Burnett won the land and the herd in a Fort Worth poker game. You can guess his winning hand.

JESSE CHISHOLM blazed the Chisholm Trail, the main cattle trail from the Lone Star State. He didn't set out to mark a trail for others to follow. He just headed for Kansas by the best route he knew—and he knew them all. Others followed, and the rest is history.

JOHN CHISUM started out as a Texas trail boss, delivering tens of thousands of cattle north. After the Navajos moved out of the Pecos River Valley, Chisum moved in. Soon he was running a hundred thousand head of cattle on a two-hundred-mile stretch of range. Known as the Cattle King of New Mexico, Chisum fought back when he believed his herd was the target of long loops. His feud with rustlers ballooned into the Lincoln County War in 1878, which made a folk hero out of Billy the Kid.

MARY EASTERLY, the Nevada cattle queen, prided herself more on quality than quantity. While her herd wasn't the biggest, it was the highest grade. Year after year her cattle received the highest prices.

CHARLES GOODNIGHT and Oliver Loving fought the Comanches and blazed the Goodnight-Loving Trail from Texas to Kansas. Known for his tenacity and ingenuity, Goodnight invented the chuck wagon. He went broke several times before enlisting John Adair, a well-padded Scotsman, to fund his dreams. Goodnight put together a million-acre ranch in the Texas Panhandle. The partnership was based on Goodnight's moxie and Adair's money, so their cattle carried the JA brand.

JOHN WESLEY ILIFF, the Cattle King of Colorado, could travel from the town of Greeley northeast to Julesburg and always stay on one of his ranches. He stood out from the crowd because he never carried a gun.

RICHARD KING. The ultimate in cattle kings, Richard King started out in life as the son of poor Irish immigrants. After being apprenticed to a jeweler, he stowed away on a steamer bound for the gulf coast. He captained steamboats, traded for the Confederates, and saved his money before he entered the cattle business. He started his empire in 1851 when he bought the 15,000-acre Santa Gertrudis ranch. By the end of the nineteenth century King was the uncrowned king of Kingsville. He owned more than one million acres on the Texas gulf coast, more than 65,000 head of cattle, and employed more than three hundred cowboys.

JOHN T. LYTLE, one of the most successful Texas trail drivers, moved almost half a million head of cattle north from Texas. His property in Kansas, Colorado, and Montana was estimated to be worth $9 million. Not bad for a man who usually slept on the ground.

MRS. MASSEY was a fortune seeker who went to Colorado as an agent for an insurance company. She married a man with 150,000 head of cattle. When Mr. Massey died, she took over. Cowboys said that she managed them better than her husband.

SAMUEL MAVERICK moved to the Lone Star State from South Carolina in the 1830s and acquired a huge herd of cattle. An iconoclast, Maverick refused to brand his cattle. Soon these "mavericks" were being branded by rustlers and rival ranchers. His name later stood for unbranded calves that had left their mothers before being branded.

Range custom later ruled that the finders of mavericks were the keepers.

JOSEPH McCOY was a big operator who shipped pigs, sheep, and cattle by carloads, but he was considered a dreamer when he suggested that the railroads build stockyards on the lines going west. The Kansas Pacific Railroad finally agreed to give him a siding if he built the yards. He selected a site in central Kansas at the frontier village of Abilene. The plains were flat as pancakes, and it was a stop on the Chisholm trail that came north from Texas. He built his yards and sent word for the Texans to come north. The next year, 1867, 35,000 head of cattle arrived. A year later, twice that many. And by 1871 a million and a half were loaded. And so was Joseph McCoy.

SHANGHAI PIERCE (Abel Head Pierce) left Rhode Island at age nineteen to get away from "too many doses of sanctimony" and landed in Texas with a nickname (he resembled a Shanghai rooster), 75¢ in his pocket, and one ambition: to get rich. When he died at sixty-six in 1900 he owned more than 200,000 acres.

Shanghai built his herd by branding mavericks. When business got too big for him to handle, he hired four brothers and taught them the maverick trade. When the brothers started mavericking for themselves on the side, Pierce rounded up a posse, captured the brothers, and hanged them.

He laid low for a while, but not for long. Pierce had a voice "too loud for indoor use" and he delighted in using it. Cowboys joked that he had his bunkhouse built three hundred yards from his house so that the wranglers wouldn't hear him whispering to his wife.

For years Pierce searched for a breed of cattle immune to tick fever. He finally found a sturdy breed in the Far East. Just before his death he introduced the Brahman breed into America.

MRS. ROGERS was the wife of a minister in Corpus Christi. He tended to his flocks, while she tended to her herds. She bought and sold the cattle, knew where to find the best grass, and could ride as well as any of her cowboys. In a short time she had transformed a few cattle into a great herd, and herself into a millionaire.

NELSON STORY engineered the first successful long-distance cattle drive. In 1866 he recruited cowboys to move 2,500 head of Texas longhorns from the Lone Star State to western Montana. Despite Indians, outlaws, badlands, distance, and snowstorms, Story got his herd through.

ANDREW VOIGT, a German immigrant, came to the Dakota Territory as a young man. With the help of his wife, family, and borrowed money, Voigt built a huge ranch where he raised Hereford cattle, Percheron horses, and sheep. One of North Dakota's premier ranchers, Voigt was known far and wide for his generosity. The Sioux Indians called him "Andrew, Big Heart White Man Can't Say No." Even his own hands referred to his ranch as the "Headquarters for Hospitality."

CATTLE KATE WATSON, a homesteader in Wyoming, had the misfortune to take up residence on land adjoining Jim Averill's store, a popular hangout for cattle rustlers. When opportunity greeted her, she answered back. She dispensed her personal favors in exchange for cattle, most of them probably stolen. When vigilantes decided to put an end to the rustling in Johnson County in 1889, they rounded up Averill and Cattle Kate and lynched them both.

A SADDLE CRITIC'S GUIDE
TO THE MOVIES

Cowboys could get along well without the movies, but what would the movies do without cowboys? Cowboy movies run the gamut from great to god-awful, and most blur the gap between myth and reality.

Filmmakers never let themselves be hampered by minor distinctions like geography. John Ford often set his movies in Texas but he rarely filmed outside of Arizona or Utah. If your idea of a western landscape is desert with red mountains in the background, you can blame Old Tucson, an Arizona movie set/amusement park where hundreds of Westerns have been filmed.

Movie cowboys do about everything except care for cattle—they fight Indians, rescue schoolteachers, shoot bandits. But tending cattle is the essence of their job description. Cowboys think most Westerns are so unrealistic, they call them horse operas or fairy tales. I can still remember when one old cowboy, Jim Mullan, walked out of the theater because the wheels on the wagons were turning the wrong way.

Still, they all agree that a good Western is as rare as surfboards in Wyoming. I've polled cowboys all over the West for their favorite Westerns. Here are their top picks:

1. **LONESOME DOVE** (1989). The hands-down favorite is Larry McMurtry's epic. "It's the best I've ever seen," raves Buzz Kirkpatrick, one of the hundred cowboys chosen to ride in Montana's Centennial Cattle Drive. Two old Texas rangers put together a herd of cattle and head north for Montana.

2. **RED RIVER** (1948). A Western Mutiny on the Bounty. John Wayne plays Tom Dunson, a pioneer rancher forced to find a market for his cattle up north. Along the trail he clashes with most of his cowboys and especially with his foster son, played by Montgomery Clift.

3. **SHANE** (1953). This is a classic Western. Shane (Alan Ladd), a former gunfighter, comes to the defense of Wyoming homesteaders being driven off their land.

4. **THE CULPEPPER CATTLE COMPANY** (1972). A teenager persuades a hard-bitten trail boss, Frank Culpepper, to take him on a trail drive and becomes a man in the process.

5. **WILL PENNY** (1968). An old beat-up cowhand, Will Penny (Charlton Heston), and two other wranglers set out to find work at the end of a cattle drive. As winter sets in, Will gets a job as a line rider. Along the way, he fights rawhiders and falls in love with a dude widow (Joan Hackett) on her way to Oregon. Is there life after the big drive?

6. **MONTE WALSH** (1970). Two old cowhands (Lee Marvin and Jack Palance) struggle to survive as the sun sets on the Old West.

7. **BIG COUNTRY** (1964). A dude goes west. An ex–sea captain (Gregory Peck) arrives in Texas to marry a rich rancher's daughter and gets involved in a family feud over water rights. Despite being hazed by the cowboys, he falls in love with the big country and buys a ranch.

8. **THE HIRED HAND** (1971). This is an offbeat western about a cowboy (Peter Fonda) who goes to work for the wife he once deserted.

9. **LONELY ARE THE BRAVE** (1962). Kirk Douglas plays a maverick cowboy who's been smothered by modernization. He busts out of jail and takes off on his horse, pursued by a gum-chewing sheriff (Walter Matthau).

10. **HIGH NOON** (1952). Gary Cooper plays an ex-marshal whose wedding day is marred by the arrival of a killer that he sent to prison. His Quaker bride (Grace Kelly) tries to persuade him to leave town before the noon train arrives, but the lawman can't turn his back.

11. **RIO BRAVO** (1959). This movie has everything: a good sheriff (John Wayne) doing his job against all odds, cowardly attacks by the bad guys, barroom brawls, a romance between the hero and a girl (Angie Dickinson), and a rehabilitated town drunk (Dean Martin).

12. **THE COWBOYS** (1972). An aging rancher (John Wayne) is deserted by his cowboys just as he's ready to drive his cattle to market. He's forced to hire eleven schoolboys to fill their boots. Rustlers try to take advantage of the situation, but the boys earn their spurs and are turned into men.

THE THREE BILLS

BUFFALO BILL CODY had what it took to be a great showman—chutzpah. By the time he put together his world famous Wild West Show, he'd done a little Indian fighting and cowboying, and a whole lot of buffalo shooting and boasting. Born in Iowa in 1846, William F. Cody started out as a Pony Express rider and stagecoach driver. After the Civil War he made a contract with the railroads to furnish its workers with buffalo meat. During an eighteen-month period, Buffalo Bill killed 4,280 buffalo, an average of almost 8 a day . When challenged to defend his title, he killed 69 buffalo in an afternoon. Cody's reputation grew when he took a job as an army scout in the fights against the Cheyenne and Sioux. After killing Chief Yellow Hand, Cody was lauded for "taking the first scalp for Custer," who eventually lost his own. In 1883 Bill hired real cowboys and Indians and organized

★ Buffalo Bill Cody.
(Buffalo Bill Historical Center) ★

his famous Wild West Show. With thigh-high boots and shoulder-length hair, Cody was his own best advertisement. Dudes flocked to see Cody's crew of sharpshooters and trick-riders. Buffalo Bill revitalized the image of the cowboy. Late in life he had a change of heart and started raising, rather than killing, buffalo. That act helped save the buffalo from extinction. When the government started the bison preserves, Cody had the third-largest private herd.

WILD BILL HICKOK, the prototypical quick draw, started out as a stage driver for the Overland Stage Route. While he was hired to guard the company's horses he killed three men who wanted to clean the station out. He served during the Civil War as a scout and sharpshooter, and his reputation grew. There were lots of wild stories about Wild Bill (whose brother Lorenzo was known as Tame Bill). He could outshoot a man even when he gave him a head start. When the cow towns sprang up in the 1870s, Wild Bill became a town marshal, first in Hayes City and later in Abilene, until the voters decided he was trigger happy. A bit of a dandy, he wore his hair long and carried his six guns in the waistbands of his trousers, butts pointing inward for a better double draw. His last career was as a sharpshooter in a western theatrical thriller. But he quit when criticized for firing too close to the moccasins of dancing Indians. Some say that he had a love affair with the cowgirl tomboy Calamity Jane and fathered a child. Wild Bill, an avid gambler, ended his life at a card table. Jack McCall walked up behind him and shot him in the back of the head. He was killed instantly but still had enough time to partly pull his gun from his holster. His poker hand, aces and eights, became known as the Dead Man's hand.

BILLY THE KID was cattle country's Dr. Jekyll and Mr. Hyde. Depending on who you talked to, the Kid was a range Robin Hood or a deranged juvenile delinquent. The peach-fuzz desperado, born in New York in 1859, was fatherless by the end of the Civil War. By the time he was seventeen, the Kid had his first notch on his belt, when he killed a thug in a saloon brawl. From Kansas he moved to New Mexico and got involved in the Lincoln County War, where he kept up his habit. He was sentenced to hang but escaped and killed two guards. He killed a government agent before being tracked down and killed by Sheriff Pat Garrett. At twenty-one, the Kid was knocking on heaven's door. He was said to have killed twenty-one men, "not including Indians and Mexicans."

CHAPTER FOUR

GOOD CHUCK

THE OLD-TIME COWBOY wake-up call consisted of:

> *Bacon in the pan*
> *Coffee in the pot*
> *Get up an' get it*
> *Eat it while it's hot.*

If he was in a bad mood, the camp cook, known as Cookie, would call the cowboys to eat by yelling something like "Come and get it, or I'll throw it in the creek." He needn't have worried: The chuck wagon was the only game on the range. A traveling cafeteria, the chuck wagon was invented by trailblazer and pioneer rancher Charles Goodnight, who took a government wagon and turned it into a cowboy Winnebago. Supplies, tools, bedding, and barrels of water were stored up front. In the rear stood the chuck box—the range kitchen, with its fold-down table. Drawers and shelves held groceries, cooking utensils, tin plates, and eating irons. The Dutch oven was the cook's jack-of-all-trades, used to fry steaks, bake biscuits, simmer stews.

The heart of every cow outfit, the chuck wagon was referred to simply as "the wagon." It was the cowboys' commissary, locker room, hospital, tack room, post office, and social club. If a drifter was looking for work he would ask, "Where's the wagon?" When a cowboy threw his bedroll onto the wagon, he pledged his allegiance to the outfit and its brand. He might cuss the cook or grumble about the trail boss in private, but he would fight an outsider who insulted his outfit.

Around the wagon, the cook's word was law. Cookie was the king of chuck, the sultan of skillets, the baker of biscuits, the bearer of bandages, simply the most important guy in any cattle outfit. Even the cow boss wouldn't think of tying his horse to the wagon's wheel—unless he wanted horsehair in his beans. No cowboy could do a good day's work on an empty stomach, which is why a good cook was paid good wages—sometimes twice what a cowboy made. Range cooks developed a universal reputation for crankiness. They should be forgiven, considering their working conditions. Cooks led a solitary life, never enjoying the camaraderie that existed among the cowboys. Many cooks were old cowboys, too stove up to ride any longer, which could make a man cranky. Also, they were always battling the elements—cooking in the rain, coping with the wind, fighting bugs and limited supplies. Fuel was always short—or it was wet. That's why some enterprising cook got the idea of stretching a green cowhide under the wagon and

Cowboy Wisdom

A man can't work well on poor feed.

For a good stew, throw everything into the pot but the hair and horns—and holler.

★

★ The heart of every cow outfit was the wagon.
(*Montana Historical Society*) ★

CHUCK WAGON ETIQUETTE

These unwritten rules were strictly followed:
1. No one eats until Cookie calls.
2. When Cookie calls, everyone comes running.
3. Hungry cowboys wait for no man. They fill their plates, fill their bellies, and then move on so stragglers can fill their places.
4. Cowboys eat first, talk later.
5. It's okay to eat with your fingers. The food is clean.
6. Eat with your hat on.
7. Don't take the last serving unless you're sure you're the last man.
8. Food left on a plate is an insult to the cook.
9. Don't even think of going back to work without putting your dirty dishes in the wreck pan (the dish pan).
10. No running or saddling a horse near the wagon. And when you do ride off, ride down wind from the wagon.
11. If you empty the water bucket, refill it—pronto.
12. If you're refilling your coffee cup and someone yells "Man at the pot," you're obliged to serve refills.
13. If you come across any decent firewood, bring it back to the wagon.
14. If you ride by the campfire and Cookie's nowhere in sight, stop and stir the beans.
15. Strangers are always welcome at the wagon.

fastening it by the corners. This "coonie" or "possum belly" carried any dry wood or cow chips found along the trail.

"A roundup cook is a sort of human that was kicked in the head by a brindle cow or a cross-grained mule when very young," wrote one cowboy in the *Prescott Courier.* "Nobody with good sense could be a roundup cook. Takes a special talent to wrangle Dutch ovens and feed fifteen or twenty men that eat like walruses all hours of the day or night, rite through wind and dirt, snow, cold, rain, and mud, an' git the job done. They're temperamental as women too; an' like the bosses, don't need to sleep neither. Also, they is very cranky. The breed is fast dyin' out; they can't stand domesticating."

Cookie's menu seldom varied. It was mostly beans, biscuits, and beef. Coffee was a staple and served "barefoot," without cream or sugar. "The chuck is mainly beans, dried prunes, rice, syrup, biscuits, coffee, and lots o' salt pork," explained an Arizona cowboy. "Some outfits even furnish sugar and beef; but the boss sez these all went broke." Despite the scarcity of eggs and milk, cooks prided themselves on their baking. But overall, trail grub was hearty but simple fare, seasoned with not much more than skunk eggs (onions) and a salty sense of humor.

Cowboy Wisdom

Only a fool argues with a skunk, a

mule, or a cook.

You can judge a man by the horse

he rides, you can judge a cow outfit

by the grub it serves.

★

B E A N S

A cowboy would have starved if it weren't for his beans. They ate beans morning, noon, and night. More than one old cowboy song told what cowboys thought about the ubiquitous bean, as in:

Oh, it's bacon and beans most every day
I'd rather be eatin' prairie hay
Coma ti-yi-yippie ya yippie ya
Coma ti-yi-yippie yippie ya.

In the Old West, any cook who couldn't cook beans wasn't considered much of a cook. Cowboys say that the secret to cooking beans is to never add cold water to the simmering beans. It will make them tough. Always add boiling water. As fond as they are of beans, some cowboys refer to beans as deceitful beans cause they talk behind your back.

P O R K   A N D   B E A N S

2 lbs. pinto beans
2 lbs. salt pork, cubed
2 onions, chopped
4 Tbs. sugar
Salt to taste, just before serving

Wash the beans and pick out the stones so that no one breaks a tooth. Soak overnight. Drain, cover with fresh water, and place on a slow fire to cook. After three or four hours, add the salt pork, onions, and sugar to the pot. Keep the water level one to two inches above the beans. Never cook beans less than all morning, and it's best to cook them all day. But don't cook them into a muck.

BISCUITS

Cowboys preferred sourdough bread to anything. They would eat baking-powder biscuits or buttermilk pancakes if they had to, but they always had a craving for sourdough. A cook's first job was finding the right keg and making the sourdough starter (4 cups flour, a dash of salt, enough water to make a medium-thick batter). Once the starter had developed a thick crust around the edges, said to give the mix its distinctive flavor, a cook would defend his keg with his life. The keg was kept in the sun during the daytime, and wrapped in a blanket at night to keep the batter warm and working. On cold nights Cookie took the keg to bed with him.

SOURDOUGH BISCUITS

2 cups of sourdough starter
1 Tbs. sugar
1 tsp. salt
1 tsp. baking soda
2 Tbs. bacon drippings
2–4 cups of flour

Blend well and work in enough flour to make a soft dough. Knead lightly. Pinch off dough the size of horse apples and roll into biscuits. Place together in a well-greased Dutch oven, then turn over so greased side is up. Let rise in warm place for half an hour. Cover and bake for 30 minutes over moderate fire. When done, biscuits should be golden on top and give a hollow thunk when you tap them.

When cowboys needed meat, they killed a steer. The first night everyone might eat thick fried steak. But when a cook yelled "Grab a plate and growl," it was a sure sign that it was time for something that was all guts and no growl. Known as "Son-of-a-Bitch Stew," it has as many names as it has ingredients.

That's because it was a cowboy custom to name the dish after someone they had a grudge with, such as forest ranger stew, game warden stew, or gambler stew. But naming the stew after the cow boss could get a hand fired. In mixed company, this calf ragout was referred to as son-of-a-gun stew.

SON-OF-A-BITCH STEW

Kill a beef and take the guts: liver, heart, brains, sweetbreads, kidneys, and marrow-gut. Wash them well and cut into small pieces. Put them in a Dutch oven with a small piece of suet. Cover with water. Season with salt and pepper. Add chili pepper if you don't like the taste of guts. Boil until the meat is tender. The longer it cooks, the better it eats. Growl and serve.

COWBOY COFFEE

COWBOYS BELIEVE IN BOILED COFFEE A BIT ON THE STRONG SIDE

EGGSHELL ADDED TO BOILED COFFEE TAKES OUT BITTERNESS

TOO STRONG

FREE 5 LB.

1-HANDFUL COFFEE = 1-CUP COFFEE

CONDENSED MILK

COWBOY "COW"

JUST RIGHT

THE BIG FOUR

It took a lot of Texas land to support one cow, which is why Texas was the birthplace of some of the biggest and best-known ranches. When cowboys threw their bedrolls onto the wagon, they pledged their loyalty to the brand burned into its sides. Of all the outfits, early-day cowboys aspired to ride for these four brands.

GOODNIGHT RANCH

JA

KING RANCH

The Running W

Cowboys can thank Charles Goodnight for blazing trails and for preserving the buffalo. Goodnight went broke several times before he finally made good in the Texas Panhandle. With the backing of John Adair, a wealthy Irishman, Goodnight took over the entire Palo Duro Canyon, built up a herd of cattle, and made a profit. The JA owned about one million acres, but its 100,000 cattle grazed on another 19 million acres of public land, where buffalo also ranged. Goodnight preserved a small herd and even attempted to cross a buffalo with a polled Angus. The offspring, called a cattalo, looked great, but they were sterile and couldn't reproduce.

Richard King started his dynasty in 1853 when he purchased a Spanish land grant of 15,000 acres on Santa Gertrudis Creek near present-day Kingsville, Texas. Much of the ranch's success came from King's interest in conservation and cattle breeding. When he wasn't buying up more land, he was figuring out how to make it more productive. The ranch produced a new breed of cattle, the Santa Gertrudis, when it crossbred Brahman with Shorthorns. The ranch eventually covered 1.25 million acres, equal to half the area of Delaware.

A cowboy could ride for days and not leave the King Ranch. One cowboy put it this way:

The sun's done riz and the sun's done set
An' I ain't off the King Ranch yet.

MATADOR RANCH

The Flying V

The Matador Ranch was born when two cowboys bought range rights to a large area of the Texas Panhandle from a buffalo hunter. The two raised a herd of 8,000 cattle until 1882, when they sold the spread to the Matador Land and Cattle Company, a Scottish company with millions to plow into land and cattle. Under the watchful eye of Murdo Mackenzie, the Matador grew into a giant. Two years later the investors owned 75,000 head of cattle and 375,000 acres. And that was just the beginning. The ranch grew by leaps and bounds, eventually covering 830,000 acres in four Texas counties and 200,000 acres of leased land in South Dakota and Montana.

XIT RANCH

XIT

The 3 million-acre XIT, which stood for "Ten in Texas," was one of the most extraordinary Texas ranches. It was owned by a group of Chicagoans who, cowboys boasted, eventually learned to tell the difference between a horse and a cow. The dudes got into the cattle business by accident. In the 1870s, the new state of Texas offered to deed a huge block of the Panhandle to anyone who would build the capitol building it had on the drawing boards. Three wealthy businessmen and one builder, none of whom had ever even seen the Panhandle, accepted the proposal. The speculators planned to recoup the construction costs, roughly $3 million, by subdividing the land. When no buyers materialized, the owners decided to fence the ranch and go into the cattle business. They stocked it with 150,000 head and hired B. H. Campbell to run it. Campbell was infamous for the ranch handbook that he passed out to all new hands. The XIT rules prohibited cowboys from carrying guns, playing cards, or spurring horses in front of the saddle. By 1901, the XIT's days were numbered. The owners, who had never gotten as much as a porterhouse steak out of it, decided to sell out.

CATTLE COUNTRY

WHEN MOST DUDES think of cattle country, they think of somewhere west of Chicago and east of California, with a whole lot of nothing and a homogeneous population. They are both right and wrong. "Where does the West begin?" dudes ask. One hard-boiled cattleman has this answer: "Where your land is so poor, season so short, water so scarce that you can't do anything but raise cattle, that's the West." Arthur Chapman answered with a poem:

Out where the handclasp's a little stronger,
Out where the smile dwells a little longer,
That's where the West begins.

Many cowboys agree that the West has no boundaries, that it's a state of mind. The West tends to think of itself as a single place, starting somewhere between the Mississippi and the Front Range of the Rocky Mountains. The western boundary is the Cascade Mountains of Oregon and Washington and the Sierra Nevada of California. California is the coast, not the West.

Cowboy Wisdom

Never approach a bull from the front, a horse from the rear, or a fool from any direction.

Every old son of a gun is a buckaroo at heart.

★ A buckaroo quartet. (*Robin Barker*) ★

Bob Athearn, a popular historian, used to say, "I wouldn't let California into the West with a search warrant." Many cowboys agree. If you ask an Arizona cowboy where he's from, he'll probably answer "the West." The exception, of course, is Texans, who reserve the right to be chauvinistic. Regardless of where they're from, cowboys think of their home range as "God's country."

God's country is high, wide, and handsome. It's a land of unbounded plains, towering mountain peaks, grand canyons, blistering badlands, where the number of livestock dwarfs the number of people. In many places a cowboy can ride off into the hills and never meet another soul until he returns home at night. In Wyoming, there are just over five people per square mile. The same goes for Montana. Nevada and the Dakotas have fewer than ten people per square mile. That translates into plenty of elbow room, something that cowboys cherish.

Time moves a little slower out west. There's so little human contact that cowboys savor encounters at the feed store, linger over coffee at the local diner, chew the fat with a neighbor, greet the mail man like he's Santa Claus.

Cowboys have always called it like they saw it. The Old West was a land where "there are more cows and less butter, more rivers and less water, and you can see farther and see less, than any country in the world." It still rings true.

Cowboy Wisdom

You can take the cowboy out of the country, but you can't take the country out of the cowboy.

Better for a man to wear out than rust out.

Minding one's own business is the best life insurance.

★

BUNKHOUSE READING

When I was a girl, one of my chores was sweeping out the cowboy's bunkhouse once a week, whether it needed it or not. At boot camp, young soldiers have to submit to weekly inspections. At cow camp, young cowboys are left alone, which means the bunkhouse will look like a tornado went through it.

The bedside tables will be littered with reading material, mostly magazines and paperback novels. Their favorite authors? Louis L'Amour (*Conagher* and *The Broken Gun*), Will James (*Horses I've Known* and *All in the Day's Riding*), and Larry McMurtry (*Leaving Cheyenne* and *Lonesome Dove*). Popular magazines? *Western Horseman*, *ProRodeo Sports News*, *Hoof and Horns*, *Beef Today*, *Rope Burns*, *Horse & Rider*, *Ropers Sports News*, and *Cowboy Magazine*.

★ Fourth-generation California ranch. (*Julie Chase*) ★

COWBOY CELEBRATIONS

Whether it's called a fiesta, a rendezvous, a roundup, a fandango, a jamboree, or a gathering, cowboys will be there. Probably because they lead such solitary lives, cowboys love to celebrate. Every range has must-see events that cowboys and their families go to year after year. Most cowboy celebrations revolve around rodeos, roundups, livestock sales, and state fairs. They are not sedate affairs. My uncle tells a tale about an old cowboy he ran into at the Cheyenne Frontier Days. "Where are you staying?" Uncle Bill asked his old friend. "Staying?" answered the cowboy. "I'm only going to be here three days."

Here's a list of some of the highlights on the cowboy's social calendar:

COWPUNCHERS

January   Southwestern Exposition and Stock Show Rodeo   Fort Worth, TX

February	San Antonio Livestock Exposition Rodeo	San Antonio, TX
May	Cowboy Symposium and Celebration	Lubbock, TX
August	Dodge City Days	Dodge City, KS
September	Tri-State Fair	Amarillo, TX
September	Bolo Ball	Oklahoma City
November	National Cutting Horse World Futurity	Fort Worth, TX

C O W B O Y S

January	National Western Stock Show and Rodeo	Denver, CO
May	Miles City Bucking Horse Sale	Miles City, MT
June	National College Rodeo Finals	Bozeman, MT
July	Calgary Stampede	Calgary, AB
July	Cheyenne Frontier Days	Cheyenne, WY
July	Great Pikes Peak Cowboy Poetry Gathering	Colorado Springs
July	Last Chance Stampede	Helena, MT

V A Q U E R O S

January	Red Bluff Bull Sale	Red Bluff, CA
February	La Fiesta de los Vaqueros	Tucson, AZ
June	California Cowboy Show	Carmel, CA
July	California Rodeo	Salinas, CA
October	Lincoln County Cowboy Symposium	Ruidoso, NM
November	Ranchers Day & Vaquero Show	Murieta, CA

B U C K A R O O S

January	Cowboy Poetry Gathering	Elko, NV
May	Jordan Valley Big Loop Rodeo	Jordan Valley, OR
July	Snake River Stampede	Nampa, ID
August	Caldwell Night Rodeo	Caldwell, ID
September	Pendleton Roundup	Pendleton, OR

★ A well-earned saddle break. (*John Morris*) ★

Muley	= a steer without horns
Mustang	= a wild horse
Near	= left side
Nellie	= skinny old cow
Off	= right side
Off his feed	= someone who feels bad
On the hoof	= live cattle
Opry House	= the top rail of the horse corral
Outfit	= a ranch's hands and herds
Outlaw	= a horse that can't be subdued
Point rider	= cowboy who rides at the head of cattle herd and acts as pilot
Pool rider	= a cowboy who tends cattle for several ranchers on their joint summer ranges
Pounding leather	= riding hard
Pull leather	= grab the saddle horn for safety
Pull a calf	= help with its birth
Puncher	= short for cowpuncher, a Texas cowboy
Regular	= the opposite of a tenderfoot
Rig	= a saddle and all of its straps
Ridden hard and put away wet	= a horse that's been abused or a person who shows the effects of hard living
Ride fence	= check the fences for downed wire
Saddle blankets	= pancakes
Saddle tramp	= a professional grub liner
Sawbones	= doctor
She stuff	= heifers and cows, female cattle
Skirt	= the bottom leathers on a saddle
Slick	= an unbranded calf
Smooth mouth	= an old horse
Sore up	= abrasive wound caused by ill-fitting saddle or cinch
Spinner	= a bucking horse that rears up and backwards
Spread	= a ranch and all its buildings and cattle
Springing heifer	= cow about to have her first calf
Stove up	= injured or crippled
String	= lariat
Tenderfoot	= an inexperienced newcomer
Tie man	= a cowboy who ties his rope to the saddle horn
Tin belly	= cheap spur
Top	= the best, as in top hand

Tree	= the wooden frame of the saddle
Waddie	= an extra cowboy who fills in
Widowmaker	= an especially bad horse
Windies	= cattle driven out of canyons
Woollies	= sheep
Wrangler	= the cowboy who handles the horses
Wreck	= a serious riding or roping accident
Yearling	= one-year-old colt or calf

HORSE RIGGING

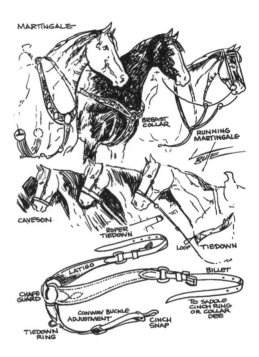

MARTINGALE

BREAST COLLAR

RUNNING MARTINGALE

CAVESON

ROPER TIEDOWN

LOOP TIEDOWN

LATIGO

BILLET

CHAFE GUARD

TO SADDLE CINCH RING OR COLLAR DEE

TIEDOWN RING

CONWAY BUCKLE ADJUSTMENT

CINCH SNAP

COWBOY CUSSING

Cowboys have raised cussing to a fine art, though you won't hear swearing much around the house or in front of women. Sometimes the words themselves aren't profane, but the meaning is plain as the nose on your face. "You can't work cattle without cussing," explained one North Dakota cowboy. "They won't move, they won't go nowhere if you don't cuss them." Profanity, the secret to getting cows to get up and git, is also a tonic for frayed nerves.

When city slickers talk dirty, they usually refer to a man's mother or the sex act. Cowboys, on the other hand, make reference to animals, particularly their hind ends. A cowboy often talks about this part of his own and an animal's anatomy. When a horse lowers his head to work up steam to buck, cowboys say that he "swallowed his ass." The condition of a cowboy's own ass, which makes direct contact with the saddle and takes the bumps and the abuse of riding, is of prime importance.

One old cowboy song, "The Old Chisholm Trail," which was said to have a verse for every mile, went:

> *My foot in the stirrup, my ass in the saddle,*
> *I'll bid good-bye to these God damn cattle.*

If a horse has an easy gait, a cowboy might joke that "he has to stop from time and time to let my ass laugh." A common expression is that one good ass can wear out three cowboys. When a cowboy is in a bad mood, he's "red assed." A sure way to insult a young cowboy is to call him a "round ass," meaning that he's lost his nerve or he's too old to ride bucking broncs.

Manure is something that cowboys are often knee-deep in. It's stepped in, kicked up by galloping horses, and used by cowboys to get their meaning across. Cowboys call rough country, like the badlands of South Dakota, "tiger shits." When a cowboy has heard enough, he won't hesitate to say "You're full of horse manure."

Cowboy Wisdom

Every jackass thinks he's got horse sense.

When you get angry, count to ten;

when very angry, cuss.

HAT'S ON

REMOVE HIS HAT and a cowboy feels naked. A cowboy in a well-seasoned hat admitted to me, "My hat's so nice, it's getting to be that I want to sleep in it." Folks say that a cowboy's hat is the first thing he puts on in the morning and the last thing he takes off at night.

Range etiquette doesn't require a cowboy to remove his hat when he enters a building. Ab Blocker, a famous Texas trail boss, wore the same style hat—a tan Stetson with a high round crown—for sixty years. Once when he

★ Cowboys wouldn't think of napping without their hats.
(*James Fain*) ★

was driving a herd from Mexico to Texas, he had to do business with Mexican border officials. A friend advised him to remove his hat before entering the customs office. "When in Rome, do as the Romans," the friend urged. "Then I'll get out of Rome," replied Mr. Ab, who kept his hat on and still got his papers.

Blocker's sentiment still lives. Walk into a steak house in Tulsa or Cheyenne or Pocatello and you'll find tables full of cowboys with napkins on their laps and

BASIC CATTLEMAN CREASE

BUCKAROO TELESCOPE CREASE IS NOW POPULAR AGAIN

SLANTED 1920 STYLE

POPULAR CUTTING HORSE STYLE

OLD STYLE MONTANA PEAK STYLE ADOPTED IN VARIOUS FORMS BY MILITARY AND LAW ENFORCEMENT GROUPS —

POPULAR WEST COAST STYLE

BLUE

CROWN

BAND   BRIM

SEWN BOUND EDGE BRIM

RAW EDGE BRIM

BRIM SHAPES

AS VARIED AS THE WEARERS

A KETTLE-CURL BRIM HAS ROUNDED EDGE KEEPING ENTIRE BRIM STIFF —

STRAW HATS HAVE SHAPEABLE WIRE IN THE BRIMS -

HAT SHAPES

hats on their heads. Knock off a cowboy's hat and he's dehorned, diminished, demoralized—and mad. Little wonder that cowboys have developed the fine art of dancing with a girl or riding a bucking bronc without flipping their lids.

At one time, all cowboy hats were called John Bs, as in John B. Stetson. Stetson, a Philadelphia hatter, made a trip out west in the 1860s seeking a cure for tuberculosis, the plague of hatters. One night Stetson made a big umbrellalike hat that he joked would be the most practical lid in the West. It was big enough to protect a man from wind, rain, flies, and foul jokes. As a prank, Stetson wore his Carmen Miranda–size hat when he rode into mining camps. One day a rugged old miner stopped Stetson on the trail and offered to buy his hat for $5. Stetson pocketed the gold and the man rode off with his new crown.

When Stetson regained his health and returned home to Philly, a city of men in pint-size derbies, he remembered the ten-gallon hat he had sold. Since the cattle trade was just getting started, he decided to gamble his health and his fortune on the cattle kings. He fashioned a big tan felt hat and gave it a big name—"Boss of the Plains." Then he sent samples to hat dealers out west and waited. Within weeks orders poured in from cowboys, trail bosses, ranchers, even Texas Rangers.

The Boss of the Plains and its descendants proved to be more than a form of plumage. It was a hat of many uses. Besides keeping the sun out

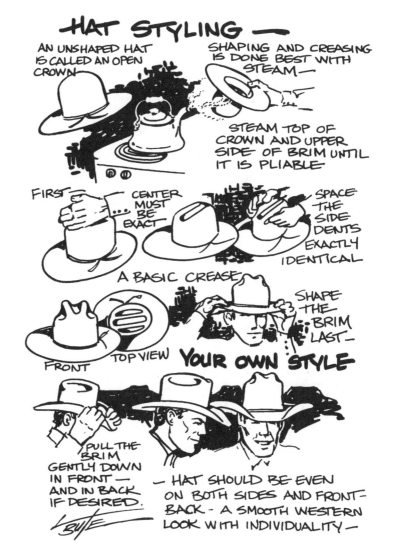

HAT STYLING —

AN UNSHAPED HAT IS CALLED AN OPEN CROWN

SHAPING AND CREASING IS DONE BEST WITH STEAM —

STEAM TOP OF CROWN AND UPPER SIDE OF BRIM UNTIL IT IS PLIABLE

FIRST

CENTER MUST BE EXACT

SPACE THE SIDE DENTS EXACTLY IDENTICAL

A BASIC CREASE

SHAPE THE BRIM LAST —

FRONT   TOP VIEW   YOUR OWN STYLE

PULL THE BRIM GENTLY DOWN IN FRONT — AND IN BACK IF DESIRED.

— HAT SHOULD BE EVEN ON BOTH SIDES AND FRONT-BACK - A SMOOTH WESTERN LOOK WITH INDIVIDUALITY —

of the cowboy's eyes or the rain from running down his neck, a cowboy hat was used to fan a fire, whip a horse, call for help, carry water.

Nothing says as much about a cowboy as his hat. It's his badge, his emblem, his signature. The color, the style, the creases all give clues to a cowboy's persona, signaling where he's from, his age, his work, his personality. Desert cowboys, for example, wear light-colored hats with high crowns, pinched in for protection from the sun. Cowboys up north favor smaller crowns dented in all around and a narrow brim because of the high wind. In wet country, hats are often creased just once down the front to form a rain drain. If a cowboy hat has a narrow brim, chances are that it belongs to a mature cowboy. Younger fellows with

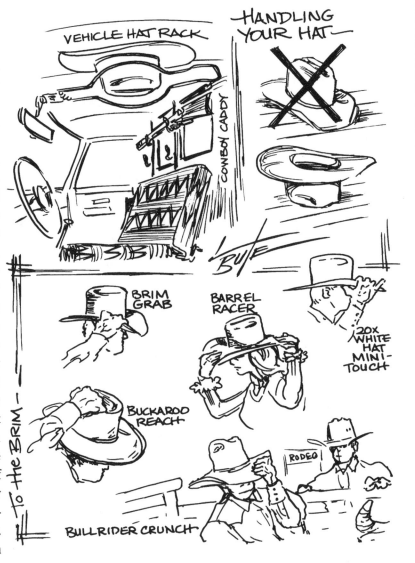

66

broader horizons like broader brims.

Rodeo riders like a cattlemen's crease with an upturned rim. A rancher will wear a cattlemen's crease with a wide flat brim. Cowboys wear hats that are curled up on the sides, probably so that they can ride three in a pickup. Buckaroos can be picked out of a crowd by their high-crowned hats and wide brims, reminiscent of the 1930s movies. Unlike cowboys, they wear stampede strings under their chins so that their hats don't blow away in high winds. Women wear hats at the ranch but they don't wear their hats to town. "I don't want to have hat hair," admits one cowgirl.

Cowboy Wisdom

A bad rainstorm will separate the men from the boys, the beaver hats from the hare hats.

Only a fool would pay money for a baseball hat with someone else's brand on it.

shape them on a fence post.

One of the best hatters around is Sheila Kirkpatrick, who makes her home and her hats in Wisdom, Montana. She got her start creasing hats for her father, a popular South Dakota rodeo announcer. Great hat creasers like Kirkpatrick, who was recently inducted into the Cowgirl Hall of Fame, know how to give you the right look. They'll start by studying your skin coloring. "The color of the hat depends on your complexion," says Kirkpatrick. "If you burn, you should stick to darker colors. A light hat will pale you out." Movie directors used to put bad guys in black hats and good guys in white, but those

When buying a hat, many cowboys head straight for the open-crown forms. They're not pretty. In fact, the cone-head crowns and flat brims look more like cigar-store Indian bonnets than cowboy crowns. But most hatophiles have them blocked and creased by a master hat creaser, who will transform the floppy felt into the pride and joy of the guy under the brim. Impatient cowboys take them home, stick them in the horse trough, and

distinctions don't hold anymore. Black is one of the most popular colors today, especially among rodeo riders and country western singers.

Hatmakers say that for a long time country western singers influenced hat styles. "Everyone wanted a low-crowned, flat-brimmed hat like George Strait or a black hat like Garth Brooks," says Tom Hirt, a custom hatter in Penrose, Colorado. "Now cowboys want their hats to look like they were purchased in the 1870s."

Most hats are a blend of beaver, rabbit, elk, and other fur. The best hats in the world are 100 percent beaver fur. Beaver hairs are tipped with microscopic barbs. When the hat felt is made, the barbs lock together, creating a smooth, fine, dirt-resistant surface.

Cowboy hats get more X ratings than dirty movies. If you look on the inside of a hat, you'll notice some X's or a number X on the sweatband. The X's stand for quality; once they stood for the amount of beaver fur in a felt. The rule of thumb is the more X's, the better the hat. A 100 percent beaver hat used to be labeled 20X, but today there is no standard X rating. Only the feltmaker knows for sure how much beaver goes into a hat. "One man's 3X could be another's 10X," says Hirt.

But even quality has its shortcomings. A beaver cowboy hat is fine in the spring and the fall when days are neither hot nor cold. But it's beastly hot in the summer and offers no protection for the ears in cold winters. About May or June cowboys

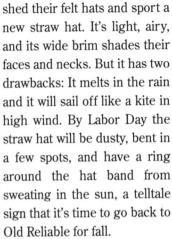

Cowboy Wisdom

Like a good cowboy, a good hat just gets better as it gets older.

Just because he's wearing a hat doesn't make him a cowboy.

★

shed their felt hats and sport a new straw hat. It's light, airy, and its wide brim shades their faces and necks. But it has two drawbacks: It melts in the rain and it will sail off like a kite in high wind. By Labor Day the straw hat will be dusty, bent in a few spots, and have a ring around the hat band from sweating in the sun, a telltale sign that it's time to go back to Old Reliable for fall.

Some cowboys wear cowboy hats all winter long, but frostbitten ears are a hazard of the trade. "When you're twenty, you'll stand a lot more abuse to keep up your cowboy image," admits one fortysomething cowboy who wears a Scotch hat with earflaps in subzero weather. Others stick with their cowboy hat but tuck a pair of earmuffs in their pockets—just in case.

Baseball caps have become popular around the corral, especially in the summertime. They don't get in the way when you're roping, and they're often free.

HOW TO CARE FOR YOUR HAT

If it's treated with love and respect, a good hat will last longer than your hairline. Here are some tips from the corral:

1.   Don't grab your new hat on the crown. Hold it on the front and back and position on your head.

2.   The safest place to keep your hat is on your head.

3.   If you must take it off, turn it upside down and set it in a cool, shady, clean place—not in a hot pickup. Don't put it down crown-side up. The brim will curl up and all the luck will spill out.

4.   If it's a good hat, it can be rained on all you want. But if you do use a rain cover, buy one a few sizes too big. It may look funky but that's better than a permanent bend or crack in the fabric, caused from a cover as tight as a Tupperware lid.

★

Cowboy Wisdom

A sure sign of spring is a

cowboy in a new hat.

★

---

5.   Don't put the cover on after it starts to rain. It will create a sauna that will ruin the hat. And when you come in out of the rain, take the cover off and let the hat air dry.

6.   Once a week or when your hat gets dusty or linty, clean it gently with a soft brush or a special hat sponge. In a pinch use a barely damp Turkish towel.

7.   Depending on its use, have your hat cleaned and recreased every six to twelve months. You'll be surprised how a hatter can breathe new life into an old friend.

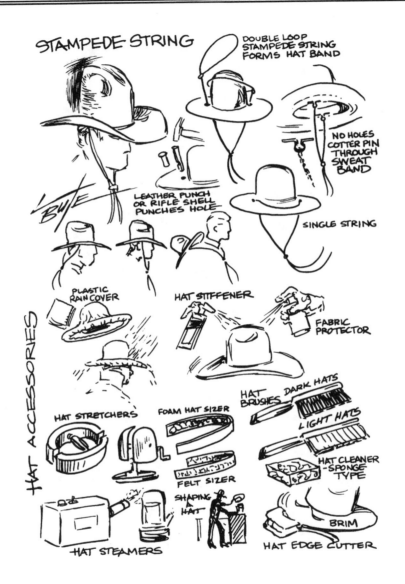

STAMPEDE STRING

DOUBLE LOOP STAMPEDE STRING FORMS HAT BAND

NO HOLES COTTER PIN THROUGH SWEAT BAND

LEATHER PUNCH OR RIFLE SHELL PUNCHES HOLE

SINGLE STRING

PLASTIC RAIN COVER

HAT STIFFENER

FABRIC PROTECTOR

HAT ACCESSORIES

HAT STRETCHERS

FOAM HAT SIZER

FELT SIZER

HAT BRUSHES

DARK HATS

LIGHT HATS

HAT CLEANER - SPONGE TYPE

SHAPING A HAT

BRIM

HAT STEAMERS

HAT EDGE CUTTER

COWBOY DUDS

★ A cowboy's most important tool is his rope. (*Julie Chase*) ★

THE WAY A cowboy looks and feels is one compensation in a trade known for its long hours and short pay. Fashion comes and goes, but cowboy clothing is timeless. It probably goes back to range traditions. Cowboys didn't have a lot of money to spend on their wardrobe, preferring to lay out any extra cash on horse tack or some new equipment. Even if he did have money in his pocket, he didn't have a lot of closet space. Most of his wardrobe was on his back. The rest was tied behind his saddle or rolled up in his bedroll. Cowboys today look to tradition for their basic sartorial direction and then add a few frills of their own.

SHIRTS

Form-fitting cowboy shirts serve a dual purpose. They accentuate a cowboy's preternaturally broad shoulders and trim waist. There's no loose fabric to get hung up on a saddle horn or a fence. A "western shirt" automatically means a shirt with two breast pockets, special wrist cuffs, and yokes front and back. The yoke is reinforced with two layers of fabric, to withstand the strains and tugs of roping. The wide cuffs ensure a snug fit at the wrist so that the sleeve doesn't slip down and interfere with roping.

Cowboy shirts are instantly recognizable by the pearl snaps. Jack

Weill, founder of Rockmount Ranch Wear in Denver, introduced pearl snaps to cowboys in the 1940s. "I wanted to create a western shirt that was distinctive," says Weill, who sensed that cowboys wanted their own special style. "I called the people at Gripper Snaps and told them I wanted to put snaps on shirts. They told me it was an incorrect application, but I said, "If I buy them, I can eat them as Post Toasties if I want to. Finally they sent me ring fasteners, just like the kind they used on baby pants. "

Weill's snappy shirts were a big hit with cowboys. As any parent knows, snaps are infinitely practical. They're faster than buttons. They're easy to open and

★ A bronc buster never stands if he can sit.
(Julie Chase) ★

close with one hand. They're also a safety net for cowboys. If a rider's shirt gets caught on a steer's horn or a fence post, the snap pops right open.

While many cowboys wouldn't be caught in broad daylight with a shirt with buttons, some cowboys are bucking tradition and switching to buttons. And here's why. In the late 1970s cowboys in Texas started buying new shirts and having them starched at commercial laundries. "They were their dress clothes, their church clothes, wedding clothes, dancing clothes, and they wanted to look sharp," says John Neal, director of western retail marketing at Wrangler. Only one problem. The big commercial presses were hell on snaps, which couldn't be replaced. "One ruined shirt and a cowboy was ready to switch

BANDANAS and WILD RAGS

BUCKAROO STYLE

36" SQUARE SILK SCARF

COWBOY STYLE

CONCHO

SQUARE KNOT

SCARF SLIDE

BRIDLE LOOP

BARRETTE

BRAIDED RAWHIDE

In the old days cowboys had two choices when they were deciding on a western shirt—solid pastels or muted plaids, what some cowboys despairingly call "farmer plaids." But today, cowboys sport shirts as bright as a desert sunset. Maury Tate, a champion calf roper from Apache, Oklahoma, was weary of the shirt selection at his local western store. "So I bought some hot pink cloth and a little black trim and took it to a seamstress," explains Tate. "I wanted it to have a standup collar and tight fitting cuffs. She made it just right, so I asked her to make me a few more." Since then Tate has created and marketed his own brand of Mo Betta shirts. They've caught on with rodeo riders as well as country western singers.

Regardless of the palette, western shirts are still judged the old-fashioned way: Will it turn a woman's head?

to buttons," says Neal. And Wrangler and many shirt manufacturers complied—in some areas. But the starch tradition really only caught on in Texas and Oklahoma. Cowboys in the northern Rockies and in Canada, where commercial laundries are as rare as a hot day in January, weren't willing to drive sixty miles to an establishment that would starch a shirt. So they've stuck with snaps.

Real cowboys don't wear short sleeve shirts. It's even written in the rodeo rule book. A short sleeve is more likely to catch on something. Since a cowboy spends most of his day outside, the long sleeve protects his arms from scratches from thick brush as well as the hot sun.

NECKWEAR

A bandana, usually red or blue, functions as a cowboy's neckwear, handkerchief, dust mask, washcloth, towel, hot pad, and tourniquet. If it's not around his neck, you can be sure that it's in his pocket. Buckaroos wear a "wild rag" around their neck. The large silk scarf may look like an ascot but it's not decorative: It keeps the north wind from whistling down his shirt.

When cowboys get dressed up, they're more likely to wear a bolo tie, a string tie held together with a silver concha or a piece of agate. Bolo ties have a mysterious origin. Some say they evolved from pigging strings, the small ropes used to tie the legs of calves in calf roping contests. Others insist that bolo ties are all about balls. The name is a corruption of the Spanish *bolas* and comes from *boleadoras*, two balled weights at the end of a forked rope, the gaucho's equivalent of the lariat. Who knows? Maybe it takes *bolas* to wear bolos.

VESTS

Whether made of elk hide, worsted wool, or goose down, cowboys wear them for extra warmth and extra pockets. Where else is he going to put his cigarettes, tobacco, matches, pocket knife, keys, pills, wallet? Only a fool would ride a horse with bulging pants pockets.

JACKETS

Hollywood cowboys love fringed jackets but no self-respecting cowboy would ride in long fringe—too big a risk that the fringe will get caught in his rigging. If they do favor fringe, they save it for Saturday night.

In the Southwest, cowboys wear denim jackets. But in colder climates working hands like to pull on a Carhartt, a long heavy brown canvas jacket with a zipper, not buttons. The blanket lining keeps them extra warm.

On rainy days, cowboys slip into slickers or dusters, those long old-fashioned raincoats.

Some cowboys have taken a fancy to satin baseball jackets. They're particularly popular when embossed with the name of the local saddle club or the emblem of their rodeo event. The most prized jacket is a rodeo jacket that sports the emblem of the NFR, the super bowl of rodeos. They're the the letter jackets of the cowboy world.

JEANS

They're as American as apple pie, but jeans were invented by a German immigrant. Levi Strauss sailed for San Francisco, armed with dry goods including canvas for tents and covers for Conestoga wagons. He planned to open a dry goods business. The only problem was that by the time Strauss's boat docked, he had sold out most of his merchandise, except the heavy brown canvas. He headed for the hills with his canvas, intent on peddling it to miners who had struck gold in the 1849 Gold Rush.

"You should have brought pants," the miners told him when he made his sales pitches. "Pants don't wear worth a hoot in the diggings." Not one to be discouraged, Strauss took his canvas to a tai-

BLUE JEAN ETIQUETTE

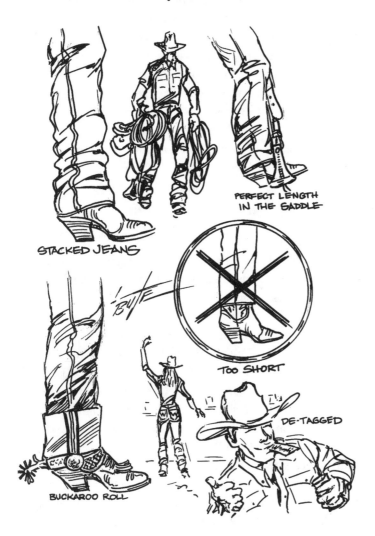

STACKED JEANS

PERFECT LENGTH IN THE SADDLE

TOO SHORT

BUCKAROO ROLL

DE-TAGGED

lor and created the world's first jeans. Soon Levi was sold out and word had spread among the miners that Levi's pants were damn near indestructible. The sailcloth made the pants tough and the copper rivets kept the pockets from ripping when they were stuffed with ore samples. When he had run out of canvas Strauss switched to a heavy fabric made in Nîmes, France, soon known worldwide as denim.

At one time all cowboys wore Levis. The heavy fabric was just right for the corral and the stable. But to satisfy cowboys, the company made a few changes over the years. The copper rivets, which had a bad habit of scratching saddle leather, were covered. Then there was the "hot rivet syndrome." When cowboys squatted too close to a roaring camp fire, the copper rivet at the base of the fly tended to heat up. When one of the company's presidents experienced the hot-rivet problem firsthand, he banned it.

Cowboys introduced dudes to Levis at the dude ranches that sprang up all over the West in the 1940s. The dudes went home toting a pair of Levis, taking a bit of the West back across the Mississippi. That's why most dudes think that cowboys wear Levis. But they're dead wrong. "The perception all over the world is that Levi is the cowboy jean," says Judy McFarlane, owner of Montana Broke. "But Wrangler is really the cowboy jean." McFarlane made a hit on the East Coast when she began peddling used cowboy jeans—Wranglers, of course. Each pair of jeans came with a tracking guide explaining the origin of each stain or rip or sign of wear.

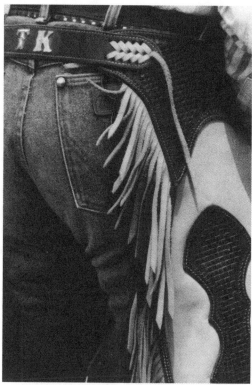

★ The chaps are custom, the pants are Wranglers. (*Vicki Anderson Shampeny*) ★

Levis may have been the first jeans, but McFarlane is right. A real cowboy's first choice is Wrangler. Little wonder. Wrangler's jeans were designed by cowboys—for cowboys. The only jeans available after World War II were boxy jeans, too baggy for the taste of the Western movie stars. So John Wayne and Tom Mix and Hopalong Cassidy started having their cowboy duds custom made by a Philadelphia tailor. Before long, a lot of rich ranchers were making tracks for Philadelphia to see the tailor, who became known as Rodeo Ben.

The fellows at Blue Bell Bib Overalls saw a trend in the making. They went to Rodeo Ben and asked him to design a jean that could be mass produced for working cowboys. To help with the job, the company's new division, known as Wrangler, put together a

BELTS

TAPERED STYLE - 3 PIECE BUCKLE SET

STRAIGHT STYLE - TROPHY BUCKLE

RANGER STYLE - 4 PIECE BUCKLE

FLORAL TOOLED BUCKSTITCHED

BASKET STAMPED RAWHIDE LACING

SILVER BUCKLES

SOLID STERLING SILVER - THE BEST

OVERLAY STERLING

THIN SILVER OVER BASE

LOWER PRICED

"GERMAN SILVER" IS REALLY NICKEL

JEWELERS BRONZE ROPE EDGE AND FIGURES

SMALL NAIL ATTACHES SILVER TIP

NAME LEATHER TOOLED OR SILVER LETTERS

BELT SIZE NEXT SIZE ABOVE JEANS

J-B 30/32 40/42

THE RIGHT BUCKLE MAKES YOU FEEL 10 FEET TALL

SOME COWBOYS PREFER SUSPENDERS WHEN RANCH RIDING

consumer group of cowboy consultants like Hopalong Cassidy and Casey Jones and some rodeo rookies like Jim Shoulders, Casey Tibbs, Freckles Brown, and Deb Copenhaver. "We told them to design a jean we can sell to all cowboys," says Wrangler's John Neal. The cowboys put the jeans right to the test, astride bucking broncs and bad-tempered bulls. "It took Rodeo Ben a while to get it right," says Neal. "But on his thirteenth try, the cowboys said this is the jean that we want." In 1947 the company introduced its cowboy-cut jean, known in-house as the 13MWZ (short for thirteenth prototype men's western jean with zipper). The cowboy-cut jean took rodeo by storm. The cowboys referred to it as the Pro Rodeo jean and the PRCA endorsed it as its official jean. Almost overnight 99 percent of rodeo cowboys were wearing Wrangler jeans.

What's the big deal about cowboy-cut jeans? Well, until Rodeo Ben came along, jeans had buttons rather than zippers. And then there's that extra room in the seat and thigh, making it a lot easier to get on and off a horse or run after a steer. They also have higher back pockets so a cowboy doesn't sit on his wallet when riding a horse. The wide space between the front belt loops easily accommodates the big belt buckles that cowboys are so fond of. The legs are wide enough to fit over a boot but narrow enough to stack. Stacking is a western tradition. Cowboys buy their jeans with inseams about four inches longer than normal so that their pants legs cover the tops of their boots when they ride. No cowboy wants to be caught wearing "high-water pants." When the cowboy is on the ground, the extra length layers on the boots from the knee down. It also drags in the back, which is why the back of a cowboy's pants cuffs are all frayed.

Another telltale sign of a cowboy is the faded circle on the back pocket of his jeans. It's the unmistakable imprint of a can of chewing tobacco. Copenhagen is the most popular brand. There's no denying that cowboys spit—a lot—and when they're trapped indoors, they have a bad habit of leaving their tobacco plugs in the drinking fountains.

BELTS

Cowboy belts are more than something to hold up pants. Adorned with elaborate tooling, the cowboy's name, or fancy stitching, the wide leather strip is an expression of a cowboy's vanity. It's also a totem that shows his credentials; the bigger the buckle, the better the cowboy.

The telltale sign of a rodeo champ is a buckle the size of a steak platter. Rodeo buckles are not shy, retiring things. Not only are they big. They glitter with overlaid gold lettering and precious stones. They sparkle with engraving—the cowboy's name, his event, the name of the rodeo, and the year. Like war heroes with a chestful of medals, rodeo champs have a drawerful of buckles. To the neophyte, they might seem tacky. But in the cowboy world, they're trophies.

GLOVES

You rarely see a cowboy without a pair of leather gloves—for protection against cold, scratches, and rope burns. If they're not on his hands, they're sticking out of his hip pocket or tucked into his belt. But some stoics ride bare-handed, insisting that it's cheaper to grow skin than to buy it.

A BLUE JEAN TRACKING GUIDE

The wear and tear on a pair of blue jeans tells something about the cowboy inside. The folks at Montana Broke, a purveyor of "distressed" blue jeans, created this guide to help dudes read the tracks:

- **"L" shaped rips and various gouges.** Barbed wire fences are especially tough on jeans, as are worn-out pickup seats, bull chutes, and brush.

- **Frayed hems.** In order for the pants to be long enough when seated on a horse, the cowboy wears 'em a tad too long for walking. They skim the ground when he walks, fraying the hem in the back only. Oftentimes the cowboy will intentionally hook the hem of a new pair of pants under the heel of his boot to wear the edges faster and have that customized look within the first day.

- **Well-worn area on upper leg.** Stacking and carrying baled hay puts lots of wear on the knees and fronts of pants. Not necessarily wearing holes, the denim can become paper thin.

- **Holes in the knees.** Ranch work to rodeos, breaking horses to mending fence, these jeans have seen it all! A hailed-out knee on one leg or the other goes with the territory.

- **Well-worn seat only.** This individual probably spent a lot of time riding horses and wore leather chaps to protect his legs.

- **Round worn spot on one back pocket.** Unmistakably a can of chewing tobacco. Which pocket? Well, that depends on whether he's right-handed or left-handed.

- **Oil-base stains in various colors**. Small paint sticks are for marking sick calves and those that have received medication. Also, iodine, scarlet oil, purple spray, and leather oil are used . . . and spilled.

- **Worn tops of back pockets**. Some farriers stick the ends of horseshoes in their back pocket until they have the hoof trimmed and ready for the shoe. The top edge of the pocket takes a beating.

- **Worn and ragged area on inside of leg below the knee**. Farriers and cowboys alike are familiar with the rough edges of horseshoe nails. By cradling the horse's leg between his calves, the farrier positions the hoof for examination. Nails holding a horseshoe in place slide back and forth against jeans, leaving an unmistakable worn patch.

- **Pants without the tag in back**. Cowgirls make sport of tearing the tag off an unsuspecting guy's pants. If she's particularly amorous, she uses her teeth.

© Judy McFarlane, Montana Broke Jeans

TO BOOT

COWBOYS ARE NEVER going to get rich, but they'll always be well-heeled. No one loves boots more than Texans. Any time you're traveling by plane or train and see a cowboy with his boots in the hatrack and his hat on the floor, you can bet that he's from Texas. That's probably because Texas has more bootmakers per cowboy than any place on earth.

I'll never forget the first time I stumbled into the closet of my Uncle Bill, a cowboy clothes horse. There before my eyes were twenty-eight pairs of cowboy boots! When I asked around, I discovered that Bill's boot collection was not at all unusual. It's not that cowboys are compulsive shoppers. It's simply that cowboys can't bear to toss out a pair of boots that cost a month's pay.

The original horseman's boot can be traced to the horsemen of the Mongolian Steppes, who for centuries wore red-soled boots with high painted wooden heels. The heels were a mark of distinction and identified the wearer as a horseman, a notch or two higher on the social ladder than the average Mongol who walked.

Spanish conquistadores introduced riding boots to the New World. Until then, Native Americans made do with soft moccasins. Early bootmakers turned out square-toed boots that could be worn on either foot. A cowboy had to be tough as a boot to wear them. He formed them to his feet by taking a walk in the nearest creek and then wearing them until they fit—more or less.

Today's riding boots are a big improvement. The pointed toe makes it easier to slide your toe into a stirrup. The stacked heel prevents your boot from slipping all the way through the stirrup. (A cowboy's biggest nightmare is getting a

BOOT STYLES—

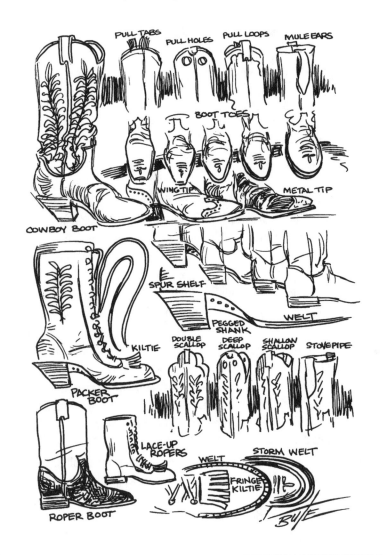

PULL TABS
PULL HOLES
PULL LOOPS
MULE EARS
BOOT TOES
WING TIP
METAL TIP
COWBOY BOOT
SPUR SHELF
PEGGED SHANK
WELT
KILTIE
DOUBLE SCALLOP
DEEP SCALLOP
SHALLOW SCALLOP
STOVEPIPE
PACKER BOOT
LACE-UP ROPERS
WELT
STORM WELT
FRINGE KILTIE
ROPER BOOT

foot caught in the stirrup when he gets thrown. It's called "getting hung up," and it can mean that a cowboy will never get up.) Bootmakers insist that the heel of the boot is slanted forward so that most of a person's weight rests on the ball of his foot, not on his instep, but some folks have other ideas. "The high heel was made to slope so far under the foot in order to leave a size-six boot print instead of a size ten!" wrote Will James, who noted that cowboys took pride in their small feet.

The general rule of heels? The shorter the cowboy, the higher the heel. But as any woman knows, footwear with high heels and pointed toes can be crippling. That's just one of the reasons why working cowboys hate to get off their horses. My brothers prefer to wear tennis shoes when they're working on the ground or rounding up horses in the corral. They pull on their boots only after the horses are all saddled up.

Just as skirt lengths have been a reflection of the state of the economy, boot heights reflect the cowboy state of mind. When boots are tall, cowboys are riding high. Buffalo Bill, the cowboy showman, wore thigh-high boots at the turn of the century when cowboys were knights in shining leather. During World War II, stay-at-home cowboys wore half-pint boots called peewees. The trend was short-lived. Peewees were catchalls for the gravel and twigs that a horse kicked up. Now that cowboys are feeling renewed pride in their ranch culture, their boots are inching up. The latest passion is for buckaroo boots,

BOOT JACK

CAST METAL ANTIQUE BOOT JACKS

TAKING OFF COWBOY BOOTS

tall riding boots that graze the knee.

With its round toe and low heel, the roper boot is the cowboy equivalent of a sneaker. Fed up with trying to run down calves while wearing high heels, ropers went to John Justin, Jr., and asked him to design a boot that they could run in. The roper has been around for almost thirty years, but it really caught on in the eighties when interest in rodeo soared. Ropers were the jocks in town and other folks wanted to emulate them.

Another special cowboy boot is the packer, the real workhorse of the boot set. The term "packer" comes from the outfitters who packed into mountains to guide vacation and hunting trips. The packer is a lace-up work boot designed for horsemen who have to get off their horses and hike or negotiate rough terrain. But it's popular among cowboys who have to slog their way through muddy corrals. Unlike a normal work boot, packers have high heels to stay on in the stirrup.

Many cowboys buy their boots off the rack

Cowboy Wisdom

Boots weren't made for

walking.

Just because a man takes

his boots off to go

wading doesn't mean

that he can swim.

A good pair of boots can

be resoled forever.

from the boot kings, Justin, Nocona, or Tony Lama, which claims to sell two boots every minute. But if he has a high instep or flat feet or bad bunions, he'll make tracks for the nearest bootmaker for a pair of custom boots. Some bootmakers will take mail orders, but cowboys stick to a bootmaker in their area so they can stomp in for a fitting. When he finds a boot that fits, he'll never change bootmakers.

When a cowboy orders a work boot, he'll choose leather that's from close to home—cowhide or horsehide. The decoration is minimal. A dress boot is a horse of a different color. Here's where a cowboy can show his spirit and endanger his wallet. Chances are that he'll pick calfskin, kidskin, or one of the exotic leathers—lizard, alligator, ostrich, snake, armadillo, kangaroo, camel, shark, antelope, and boa constrictor.

While some craftsmen like Sam Lucchese, the Matisse of bootmakers, have been bought out by big corporations, the West still boasts dozens of small bootmakers who turn out custom boots with inlays, overlays, or six rows of stitching, costing as much as a down payment on a new pickup truck. Just before the 1992 Republican convention, George Bush bought a $4,500 pair of cowboy boots from Texas bootmaker Rocky Carroll. When Texas governor Ann Richards heard that the president had bought a pricey pair of boots, she shook her head and said, "Poor George, he's all boots and no cattle."

You can tell a no-cattle cowboy a mile away. They're the ones so proud of their Technicolor rainbow boots that they stuff their pants inside their boots to show them off. The leather blossoms with flowers and birds and emblems. Walk through the Dallas airport and you'll see boots inlaid with the map of Texas, the head of a longhorn steer, or an ankle-high oil derrick. But unless you're in Texas or Hollywood, don't shotgun your pants. As a rule, cowboys are into understatement. They wear their Wranglers on the outside and their Justins on the inside.

★ Bronc riders always tape their boots before they ride. (*Vicki Anderson Shampeny*) ★

THE RIGHT FIT

Bootmaker Charlie Dunn, one of Texas's master craftsmen, used to say that he could tell from the sound of a cowboy's footsteps what was wrong with his boots. Nothing is more important—or more difficult—than a good fit. The boots may be beauties, but if they don't fit, you're in for a bout of podiatric agony.

The most common problem, according to bootmakers, is the pinching across the toe. "A boot should be snug but not uncomfortably tight," advised Dunn, who could make a leather boot fit like a silk glove.

Here are a few trade secrets from bootmakers to help get the right fit:

1. Anything over a two-inch heel may be hard to walk in.

2. Wear a thick sock when you try on boots.

3. A well-fitting boot will be comfortable immediately. There should be no breaking-in period while your foot makes peace with the boot.

4. The boot should feel snug across your instep but not tight. If your foot slips in too easily, the instep is probably too loose. Check the fit by sliding your thumb across your instep. This should cause a slight ripple of leather, but not a wave.

5. The ball of your foot should line up with the ball of the boot. If the ball of your foot is too far forward, your toes will cram into the toe box, causing the dreaded hammer-toe syndrome.

6. A steel shank in the arch of the boot gives sturdy support. That's why boots are so comfortable.

7. Your toe should be about a thumb's width back from the toe of the boot. The boot should be tight around your instep, and you should choose a toe as long as possible.

Cowboy Wisdom

You won't criticize a man after you've walked a mile in his boots.

Don't wear the same pair of boots every day. Variety not only spices up life, it prolongs it.

Nothing will cause more distress than a boot that's too short.

8. The heel of a new boot should slip a bit. After the boot is worn, the sole flexes in the ball and the slippage disappears. If there's no initial heel slippage, the boot may be too tight. Your heels will soon tell you.

9. If your feet start to burn, it's because your boots are too tight and your feet can't perspire. Remove the boots and soak your feet in epsom salts and hot water for fifteen minutes. If it happens more than once, give your boots to a smaller cowboy. Who needs cruel boots?

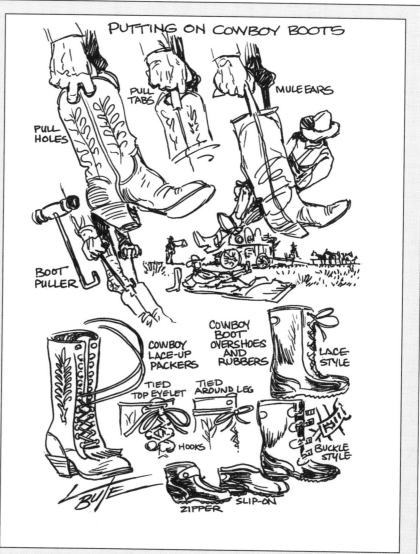

PUTTING ON COWBOY BOOTS

PULL HOLES
PULL TABS
MULE EARS
BOOT PULLER
COWBOY LACE-UP PACKERS
COWBOY BOOT OVERSHOES AND RUBBERS
LACE STYLE
TIED TOP EYELET
TIED AROUND LEG
HOOKS
BUCKLE STYLE
ZIPPER
SLIP-ON

COWBOY GEAR

ONCE HE'S DRESSED and fueled for a long day in the saddle, a cowboy straps on his outer gear. And when he rides out, there's a rope suspended from the right side of his saddle horn. It's not an ornament. A cowboy can do everything but eat with his rope. Chaps and spurs are two of the most conspicuous and most essential pieces of a cowboy's outfit. Ranch heirlooms, more beloved than the family silver, they're passed down from father to son. But there's a time and place for everything. Old-time cowhands might have worn their chaps to town because they had no place to hang them. But no modern cowboy would dream of showing up in town wearing chaps. If he's not going to saddle up, the chaps are left hanging on a nail in the bunkhouse or the barn.

★ Three generations of chaps. (*Stephen Collector*) ★

CHAPS

Here's a case where one hide protects the other. Chaps are leather leggings worn over blue jeans. Ralph Lauren paid homage to the cowboy in the late 1970s when he named his men's cologne after these twelve-hour leggings. But he taught a whole generation of urban cowboys to mispronounce chaps. They're called "shaps," not chaps. The word "chaps" is an abbreviation of the Spanish word *chapparerras,* meaning leg armor. Brush scratches, saddle sores, and bites from nasty horses were a big problem for Mexican *vaqueros* until they used a little ingenuity. They covered their saddles with cowhides, sat in the middle, and folded them over their pants to protect their legs. It did the trick, but it took so long for the rider to get tucked in that he couldn't make a fast getaway. Then

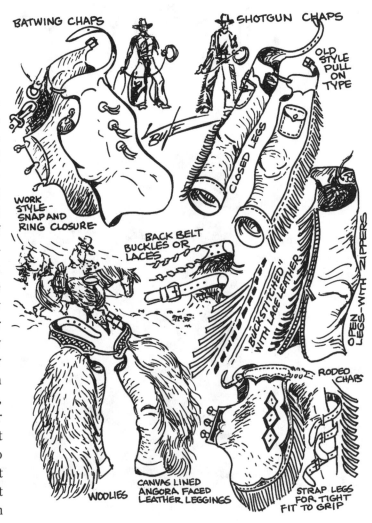

BATWING CHAPS

SHOTGUN CHAPS

OLD STYLE PULL ON TYPE

CLOSED LEGS

WORK STYLE— SNAP AND RING CLOSURE

BACK BELT BUCKLES OR LACES

"BUCKSTITCHED" WITH LACE LEATHER

OPEN LEGS—WITH ZIPPERS

RODEO CHAPS

WOOLIES

CANVAS LINED ANGORA FACED LEATHER LEGGINGS

STRAP LEGS FOR TIGHT FIT TO GRIP

some savvy rider came up with the idea of hanging the hide on the cowboy instead of the horse. As they evolved, chaps became seatless leggings made of buckskin or cowhide, held up by a belt in back and a string in front, or laced together.

Chaps look better in the saddle than they do on the ground. Open in the front and the rear, they tend to accent a cowboy's private parts. And besides, walking more than a few steps in full-length chaps is enough to make a cowboy overheat.

Today chaps come in four styles: shotgun, woolies, batwings, and chinks. They vary, depending on the climate and the terrain. Standard-issue chaps are called "shotguns" because the two narrow legs resemble the twin barrels of a double-barrel shotgun. Straight-legged so that the wind can't blow up a cowboy's leg, they sometimes have fringe sewn in the side seam. Because the sides are sewn shut, they can't be put on or taken off without taking your spurs off. Sometimes a guy ends up hopping around the corral because his boot gets stuck. That's why many cowboys have started asking for shotguns with zippers in the

★

Cowboy Wisdom

The shabbier the chaps,

the better the cowboy.

★

Don't squat with your

spurs on.

★

sides for easier exits.

Despite their usual disdain for sheep ranchers, northern cowboys have always been partial to woolies and angoras. These chaps, made from sheepskin or goatskin in the front and leather in the rear, help keep a cowboy's legs toasty warm and pad his legs in case of a bad fall. Some macho cowboys have been known to outfit themselves in bearskin, beaverskin, even wolfskin chaps. Because they're great at breaking the wind and shedding snow, hair pants are still worn in blizzard country—Montana, Wyoming, and the Dakotas. A cowboy's pride and joy is pulling on a pair of Grandpa's woolies, even if they make him look like a bowlegged animal walking on his hind legs. But they're not meant for everyday use, just days cold enough to make a polar bear hunt for cover. Fur is too hot on a warm day. A drenching rain can make a cowboy in hair pants smell like a den of unwashed wolves.

Batwing chaps, the kind preferred by Texans and most rodeo riders, are the showiest of all and the most practical. They're cooler than shotguns or woolies. They have extra-large flaps that are fastened on the side with rings or snaps, making them easy to get on without having to stop and remove your boots (one of a cowboy's most difficult jobs). Edged with contrasting fringe and decorated with silver conchas, these wide-legged chaps flap as a cowboy strides out of the arena. "Rodeo cowboys like chaps with wild flames, inlays, and long' fringe," says chapmaker Sean Schild, of Blackfoot, Idaho, who makes about 150 pairs a year. "They think that wild, flashy chaps will make their riding look better." Most working cowboys like earth tones.

Short chaps, called chinks, are spreading across the cowboy ranges like wildfire. "Chinks" comes from the Spanish *chincadera,* meaning sawed off. No one knows exactly where they come from, but these cowboy culottes are mighty popular with bucka-

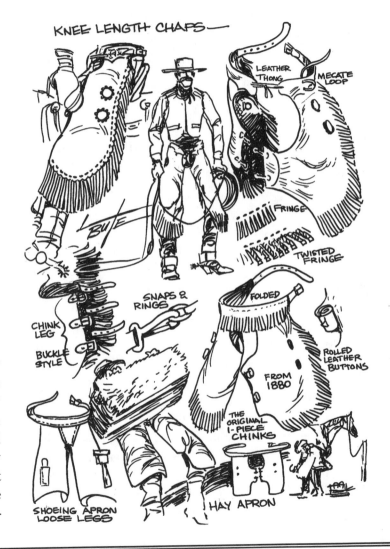

CHINKS—

KNEE LENGTH CHAPS—

LEATHER THONG

MECATE LOOP

FRINGE

TWISTED FRINGE

CHINK LEG

BUCKLE STYLE

SNAPS & RINGS

FOLDED

ROLLED LEATHER BUTTONS

FROM 1880

THE ORIGINAL 1-PIECE CHINKS

SHOEING APRON LOOSE LEGS

HAY APRON

★ Chinks are easier to work in on the ground.
(Suzanne W. Reeves) ★

thigh are high enough so that you don't sit on them. On a good pair of chinks, the fringe is cut from the leather itself, so that it cascades down the side and crosses the bottom. Fringe that is sewn on later tends to stick out like cactus spines.

SPURS

These metal hooks worn above the heel of a boot have been worn proudly by horsemen since the days of King Arthur. A sure-fire badge of a horseman, they're not just an ornament or social requirement. They're a necessity—riders find them a mighty handy way of explaining to a horse who's boss. Spurs provide a cowboy with a simple way of signaling and controlling his horse, freeing up his hands to toss a rope or hold the reins. On a well-trained horse, a cowboy rarely has to use them. The slightest movement of his leg gets his message across.

roos, the cowboy trendsetters. Just a few years ago no self-respecting Texas cowboy would wear chinks. He'd have been laughed out of the saddle for wearing high-water chaps. But they're now worn on ranges from Montana to Mexico. Chinks are cooler in hot weather and easier to get on and off.

The best chaps are custom made by experts who see that they fit like a second skin, reach high in the back around your waist, leave no gaps around your crotch, and are long enough that when you're sitting on your horse the leather still covers everything but the tip of your boot. When you stand your chaps ought to drag on the ground (most guys fold them up to keep them clean). It's also important that any buckles or snaps on the

The spur's rowels, the sharp-pointed stars, are the only thing that come between a cowboy's boot and his horse. The larger the rowel, the less cruel. It's the small thin rowel with few points that does the most damage. *Vaqueros* and buckaroos prefer

SPURS—

Cowboy Wisdom

Cowboys wear spurs in a saloon, but never in a friend's house.

★

No good man leaves spur marks on a horse.

★

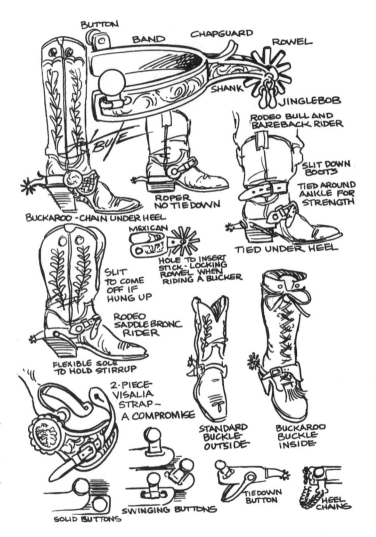

BUTTON
BAND
CHAPGUARD
ROWEL
SHANK
JINGLEBOB

BUTE
BUCKAROO - CHAIN UNDER HEEL
ROPER NO TIE DOWN
RODEO BULL AND BAREBACK RIDER
SLIT DOWN BOOTS
TIED AROUND ANKLE FOR STRENGTH
TIED UNDER HEEL

MEXICAN
HOLE TO INSERT STICK - LOCKING ROWEL WHEN RIDING A BUCKER

SLIT TO COME OFF IF HUNG UP
RODEO SADDLE BRONC RIDER
FLEXIBLE SOLE TO HOLD STIRRUP

2-PIECE VISALIA STRAP — A COMPROMISE
STANDARD BUCKLE OUTSIDE
BUCKAROO BUCKLE INSIDE

SOLID BUTTONS
SWINGING BUTTONS
TIEDOWN BUTTON
HEEL CHAINS

shiny silver spurs with large spiky rowels with up to twelve points. Northern cowboys, less showy, wear smaller rowels with fewer and rounder points. Cowpunchers like the look of gray iron, aged and rusted to a dull patina. Some even bury them to speed up the aging process.

STERLING SILVER

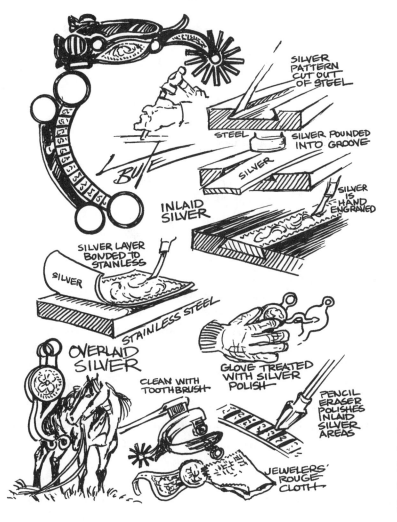

SILVER PATTERN CUT OUT OF STEEL

STEEL

SILVER POUNDED INTO GROOVE

SILVER

L BUTE

INLAID SILVER

SILVER IS HAND ENGRAVED

SILVER LAYER BONDED TO STAINLESS

SILVER

STAINLESS STEEL

OVERLAID SILVER

CLEAN WITH TOOTHBRUSH

GLOVE TREATED WITH SILVER POLISH

PENCIL ERASER POLISHES INLAID SILVER AREAS

JEWELERS' ROUGE CLOTH

When a cowboy buys a new pair of spurs the first thing he does is file the point of the rowels until they are blunt. Sharp points make the horse too nervous. One cowboy I know replaced his pointed rowels with silver dollars.

Most ranchers keep their kids in spurs and boots. But small-fry spurs don't have rowels. They'll be added later. By the time little britches can fill big britches, their spurs are as much a part of them as their hands.

There's some debate on whether spurs should be buckled on the inside or the outside. The inside looks better, but the buckle can bother the horse. Most times animal rights win out and the buckle goes on the outside. The little pear-shaped pendants that dangle from the rowel axle are called jingle bobs. Their sole purpose is to make music.

Cowboys never wear spurs inside the house because the rowels will scratch the floor and the furniture. Driving a pickup truck in spurs is a difficult trick. But some cowboys manage to never take their spurs off their riding boots. The spurs are still buckled on when the boots are cracked and worn. At the end of the day a cowboy can pull off his boots with the help of his spurs. No bootjack needed.

ROPES

Whenever you see a working cowboy on horseback, you'll see a coiled rope suspended from the right side of his saddle horn. He uses it as often as a carpenter uses a hammer. "I probably learned to rope before I learned to ride," says Jeff Griffith, a cowboy in Gallatin, Montana. "I used to drag a rope around and rope anything that stood still. Roping is just second nature to me."

But cowboys don't use just any old rope. Buying a rope is not as simple as buying tires. There are so many lengths, stiffnesses, widths, and materials available that a cowboy could own 400 ropes, each different. When a cowboy walks into a rope store, like King Ropes and Saddlery in Sheridan, Wyoming, and says that he wants to buy a catch rope, he'll be asked a few questions. Does he dally or tie hard and fast? Does he want a head

Cowboy Wisdom

Tossing your rope before building

a loop don't catch a calf.

or heel rope? A calf or steer rope? A corral or ranch rope? Is he right or left handed? "A guy may handle twenty or thirty ropes before he finds the one he's after," says Bruce King, head of King's lariat heaven. "He selects it by feel, like getting the flex of a tennis racquet." Once he's found one that feels right, he tries out the merchandise on a dummy steer in the back room.

Ropes are also called lariats, strings, lassos, or reatas, depending on who's doing the roping. *Vaqueros* and buckaroos are "dally men." They traditionally used a sixty-foot rope made of braided rawhide, called a *reata,* and swung a big loop. When they make a catch, they dally the home end of their rope loosely around the saddle horn, so they can pull it in or let out slack. "Dally" comes from *dar la vuelta,* meaning give it a few turns. Because they don't tie the rope to the saddlehorn, it can be turned loose if the roped animal tumbles into a gulch or attempts to wind up the horse and rider. Dallying takes practice but it's become standard procedure on many ranges.

Some cowboys are still "tie men." They use shorter ropes and throw smaller, more exact loops. Rather than dallying the end of their rope, they tie it tight—hard and fast—to the saddle horn. Tying hard and fast probably became a Texas tradition because good ropes were expensive. A hard-working cowboy hates to rope a steer and then have it take off toward the horizon with his rope trailing behind like a banner. It just adds insult to injury. But more cowboys have been injured from tying hard and fast than dallying. That's because if an accident happens, the rope can't be untied in a hurry.

In the old days, ropes on the west side of the Rockies were made of braided rawhide. To the east, they were made of grass. They each had their good points but both were susceptible to the weather. A

A COWBOY'S LINE

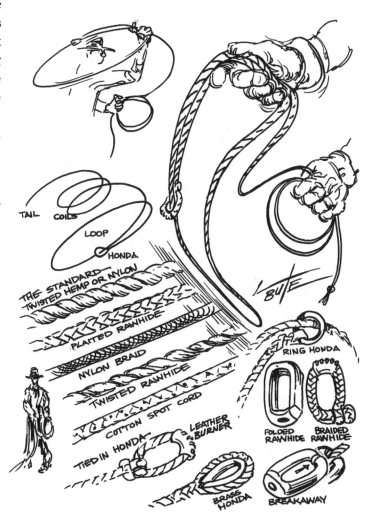

TAIL COILS

LOOP

HONDA

THE STANDARD—TWISTED HEMP OR NYLON

PLAITED RAWHIDE

NYLON BRAID

TWISTED RAWHIDE

COTTON SPOT CORD

TIED IN HONDA

LEATHER BURNER

RING HONDA

FOLDED RAWHIDE

BRAIDED RAWHIDE

BRASS HONDA

BREAKAWAY

change in humidity could take the stiffness right out of a rope, turning it limp and useless. Most ropes sold today are nylon, polyester, or a combination. Nylon ropes are more like old-time reatas and have a little bit of give in them. The rope acts as a shock absorber for the horse when a cowboy takes his dallies and the steers reaches the end of the rope. Calf ropers, who still tie hard and fast and want their critters to come to a quick stop, swing poly ropes, which are stiffer.

★ Building a loop. (*Julie Chase*) ★

The size and stiffness of a rope are crucial considerations for a cowboy. Catch ropes range in thickness from a 3/8 inch diameter rope used as a piggin' string, or kid's roping, to a 7/16 of an inch for a roper with a big paw. The small sizes are considered faster but choosing a rope comes down to finding a rope that feels good in your glove. The rope's "lay" describes its stiffness, ranging from soft to hard. Calf ropers and team roping headers prefer a softer rope so that it doesn't bounce off the head or peel off when the curl comes around. Team ropers who aim for the steer's heels pick stiffer ropes so that their ropes will stand up when they lay their trap.

Rodeo cowboys don't carry their ropes, their livelihood, around in the open air. (If a guy's carrying a rope can, you can guess that he's a calf roper.) He needs an airtight container to keep the rope as stiff as possible and still uncoil. Team ropers, on the other hand, carry theirs in nylon rope bags that look like tennis racquet covers; they prefer a softer rope, so they let it breathe a little.

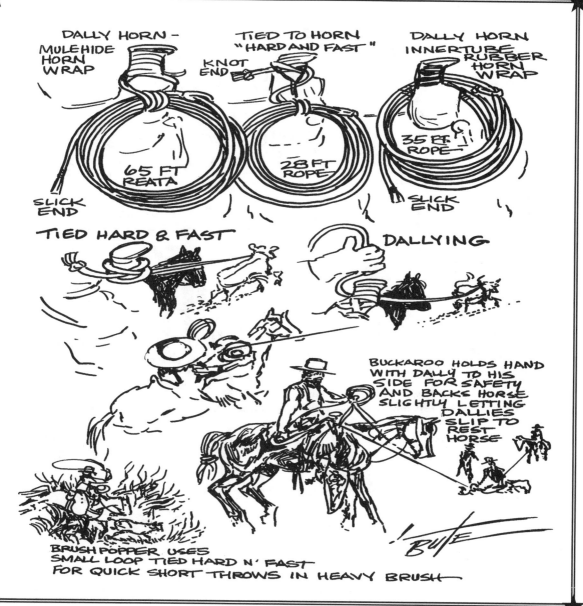

DALLY HORN - MULEHIDE HORN WRAP

65 FT REATA

SLICK END

TIED TO HORN "HARD AND FAST"

KNOT END

28 FT ROPE

DALLY HORN INNERTUBE RUBBER HORN WRAP

35 FT. ROPE

SLICK END

TIED HARD & FAST

DALLYING

BUCKAROO HOLDS HAND WITH DALLY TO HIS SIDE FOR SAFETY AND BACKS HORSE SLIGHTLY LETTING DALLIES SLIP TO REST HORSE

BRUSH POPPER USES SMALL LOOP TIED HARD N' FAST FOR QUICK SHORT THROWS IN HEAVY BRUSH

THE KING OF ROPES

A good roper can't rope with a rope right off the shelf; it's too stiff and curled. In the old days a cowboy would buy a length of rope at the hardware store, tie one end to a tree and the other to his pickup truck. He'd drive down a hill as far as he could and then leave it overnight.

Today cowboys head to King's Saddlery and King Ropes in Sheridan, Wyoming, for preseasoned ropes. King stretches its ropes the old-fashioned way. The only difference is in the quantity. Every two weeks Don King drives his tractor fitted with four spools of rope across a field. The other ends are tied to a piece of pipe. "We stretch the ropes for two or three weeks depending on the weather," says King. "Then we pull them up and cut them into standard lengths. As soon as it's emptied, the field, which will hold 28 miles of rope, is filled again.

The ropes are taken back to the shop for the final loop. The ends of the rope are knotted and seared closed with a butane torch. The rope is fitted with a honda, the knotted or spliced eyelet at the business end of a rope, for making

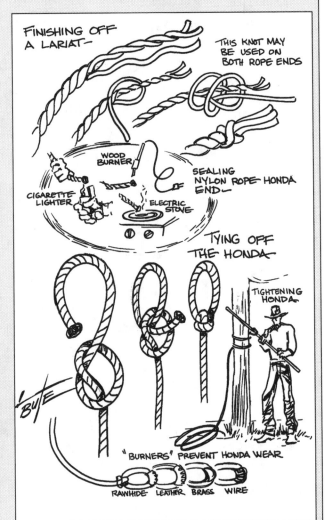

FINISHING OFF A LARIAT—

THIS KNOT MAY BE USED ON BOTH ROPE ENDS

WOOD BURNER

CIGARETTE LIGHTER

SEALING NYLON ROPE HONDA END—

ELECTRIC STOVE

TYING OFF THE HONDA—

TIGHTENING HONDA

"BURNERS" PREVENT HONDA WEAR

RAWHIDE   LEATHER   BRASS   WIRE

a loop. A small leather pad, called a burner, is tied on to protect the eye of the honda from wear and tear.

When a rope is properly stretched and ready to work it won't kink as it uncurls. Ropers say that good ropes "sing." The rope flows through the loop and makes a hissing sound as it's thrown.

Cowboy Wisdom

If the saddle creaks, it's not paid for.

★ With 400 styles to choose from, King Ropes is lariat heaven. (*King's Saddlery*) ★

HORSE TACK

OF ALL HIS gear, a cowboy is fussiest about his rig—his saddle and harnesses, bridle and reins. And little wonder. It's not unusual for a cowboy to spend ten to twelve hours a day in the saddle, so it better be comfortable. Many nights when he's slept outside, he's used it as a pillow. If not, he hangs it from a tree so that wild animals don't nibble on the saddle leathers (they like the salty flavor of sweat-soaked leather).

It's so indispens-

★ The tack room. (*Stephen Collector*) ★

able to his work that when a cowboy says, "I sold my saddle," he means that he's given up the calling and gotten a job in town. One cowboy, forced to sell his saddle to pay back taxes to the IRS, sat down and cried when the buyer walked away with his throne. It can also mean that he's lost his integrity. In *The Cowboy*, Philip Ashton Rollins tells the story of a small Montana boy who was asked by his teacher to identify Benedict Arnold.

COWBOY THRONE

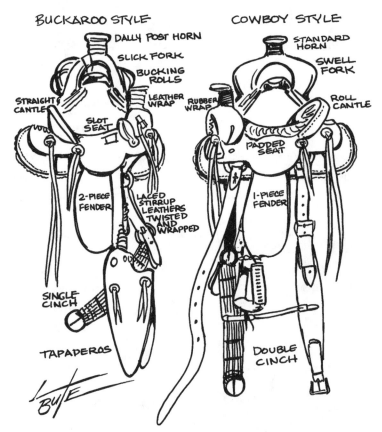

BUCKAROO STYLE

- DALLY POST HORN
- SLICK FORK
- BUCKING ROLLS
- STRAIGHT CANTLE
- LEATHER WRAP
- SLOT SEAT
- 2-PIECE FENDER
- LACED STIRRUP LEATHERS TWISTED AND WRAPPED
- SINGLE CINCH
- TAPADEROS

BUTE

COWBOY STYLE

- STANDARD HORN
- SWELL FORK
- RUBBER WRAP
- ROLL CANTLE
- PADDED SEAT
- 1-PIECE FENDER
- DOUBLE CINCH

SADDLES - A DIFFERENCE OF OPINION

The young cowboy replied, "He was one of our generals and he sold his saddle."

When a horse shows up back at the ranch with an empty saddle, the cowboys quickly form a search party to look for the rider and the wives get out their worry beads. In *The Old-Time Cowhand*, Ramon Adams explains that "an empty saddle signifies that he is either dead, hurt, or left afoot, perhaps far from home, which in itself might mean tragedy."

Buying a custom saddle is kind of a coming-of-age ritual in cattle country. Sure, dad keeps the kids in boots and some kids have a pair of pint-size chaps, but their saddles are hand-me-downs or off-the-rack models. It's only when a fellow becomes a man and is going to start to earn a wage that he'll buy a custom rig. The saddle-buying ritual is kind of a buckaroo bar mitzvah. First, he has to decide on a tree, then which kind of fork and horn, the type of skirt, what kind of stirrups he wants. Only when he's absolutely certain that he's going to make a commitment to the cowboy life does he put in his order. Good saddles don't come cheap. Cowboys used to put a $40 saddle on a $10 horse. But both horses and rigs have appreciated. A custom-made plain vanilla model made of smooth split cowhide might cost $1,500. A hand-carved saddle decorated with silver can put a cowboy back several thousand dollars. A cowboy will dig deep into his pockets for a hand-tooled leather saddle; it wears longer and is less slippery than a smooth leather seat.

A saddle is only as good as the tree it's built on. A tree is the wooden frame under all the saddle leathers. The best trees are hand-carved one at a time from select woods and

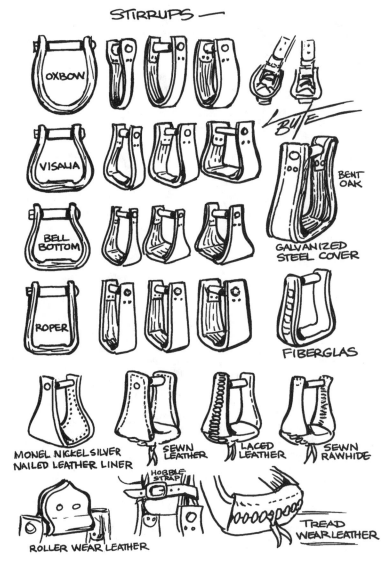

STIRRUPS —

OXBOW

VISALIA

BELL BOTTOM

ROPER

BENT OAK

GALVANIZED STEEL COVER

FIBERGLAS

MONEL NICKEL SILVER NAILED LEATHER LINER

SEWN LEATHER

LACED LEATHER

SEWN RAWHIDE

ROLLER WEAR LEATHER

HOBBLE STRAP

TREAD WEAR LEATHER

the best rawhide available. They're known by their shape as well as by the names of their makers: Tenny Haas, Sam Adams, and Shane Parker are among the best.

The front of the tree, which looks like a turkey wishbone, is called the fork. Most ropers are particular about their fork because it's where the horn, the most important part of the saddle, is attached. Swell forks—wider ones—offer more protection, but the rope can get caught under the bow. It may come as a surprise that the horn is not meant for hanging on to like a security blanket when you ride. When dudes grab the horn when they're riding a horse, cowboys joke that they're "squeezing Lizzie." To a cowboy, the horn is simply a small post for tying or dallying his rope.

The back of the tree is the cantle, the curved backrest of the saddle. Riders in flat coun-

SADDLE BLANKETS

Saddle blankets and pads protect a horse's back. A blanket drapes over a horse's back like a rug, while a pad is a stiff mat stuffed with felt or cotton. They're sometimes used together, but too many blankets can make a horse sweat and get saddle sores.

There's a little ritual that takes place at the end of every ride. After the saddle is hung back on the rack, the blanket or pad is carefully laid upside down on top of the saddle to dry out.

Polyester pads can be washed but no one does it in the family machine. Instead they sneak into a laundromat. If they have a conscience, they run the empty machine through another cycle when they're through.

It's hard to rinse detergent out of a saddle blanket. That's why many cowboys use a curry comb to clean them and then just rinse them off with a garden hose. Some cowboys take their blankets to a commercial car wash and use the pressure hoses to squirt off the dirt, sweat, and hair. Haying season, when the weather is hot and the horses aren't used much, is the best time to wash saddle blankets.

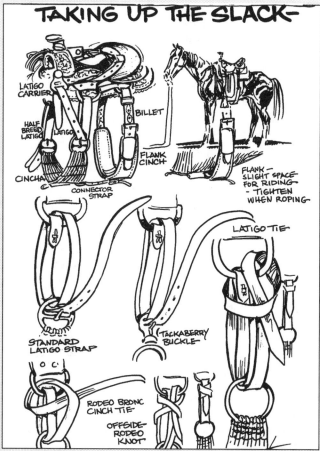

TAKING UP THE SLACK

LATIGO CARRIER

HALF BREED LATIGO

LATIGO

CINCHA

CONNECTOR STRAP

BILLET

FLANK CINCH

FLANK — SLIGHT SPACE FOR RIDING — TIGHTEN WHEN ROPING

STANDARD LATIGO STRAP

TACKABERRY BUCKLE

LATIGO TIE

RODEO BRONC CINCH TIE

OFFSIDE RODEO KNOT

try prefer low cantles, which allow the rider to move around in the saddle. They're also easier to get in and out of. Riders in mountainous terrain choose high cantles so a cowboy stays on when a horse scrambles up a steep slope. Without a high cantle, he might end up hanging on by the horse's tail.

"A good saddle should make you feel like you're sitting on a horse, not a saddle," says Jeff Schild, a saddlemaker in Blackfoot, Idaho. Besides focusing on the size and needs of the cowboy sitting in the saddle, Schild worries about the horse carrying it. "People bring their horses to the shop and we put bare trees on them to make sure that they fit," he says. "If the gullet is too narrow, the saddle will sore up a horse." A good rule of thumb: If you can put three fingers, no more, no less, between the gullet, the underside of the tree, and the horse's withers, you've got a pretty good fit.

Getting the stirrups adjusted to just the right length is an art and a science. They're perfect if you stand in the stirrups and your rear end just clears the saddle. Too much daylight under your pants and you'll fall forward when trying to post

Cowboy Wisdom

It takes a lot of wet

saddles to train a horse.

Ride the horse, not the

saddle.

★

when trotting. No daylight and your butt will feel every bump. That's why a cowboy is more likely to loan you a horse than a saddle.

Open stirrups are usually made of wood bound with iron, brass or rawhide, but sometimes all iron or brass. Buckaroos like flashy silver Monel stirrups. *Vaqueros* and cowboys in brushy country like closed stirrups called *tapaderos,* known as taps. Taps are wedged-shaped leathers that cover the front and sides of the stirrups. Theoretically, they protect a rider's boot from the brush and keep his foot from slipping through the stirrup, but it's possible that cowboys just like the way they look. The wedged-shaped piece of leather can be worked to look like the faces of bulldogs, monkeys, or eagles. The flap of the tap can be used to sort cattle, turn a young horse, or goad a slow one. If they're too long, they can catch on the brush. In wintertime, snow can build up in the toe pocket and a cowboy's boot can freeze to the tapadero.

Regardless of the style, a good saddle is tough enough to get the job done and good-looking enough to show a cowboy's pride. It's carefully crafted and even more carefully maintained.

Cowboys show their roots by how they bridle their horses. Cowboys and cowpunchers use leather bridles that go over the horse's head and ears, an iron bit that goes in the horse's mouth, and two reins that belong in the rider's hands. On the other side of the Rockies, buckaroos continue an old *vaquero* tradition and start colts with a hackamore, a bridle without a bit. The headstall is attached to a braided rawhide bosal, which fits around the horse's nose like a muzzle.

Bits come in various styles depending on how hard it is to control the horse. A bar bit is the simplest style. When the center bar is joined or linked together in the middle, the bit is called a snaffle bit. A gentle bit, it's used on young horses. A curb bit is one of the most popular styles. It allows the horse to graze but the horse

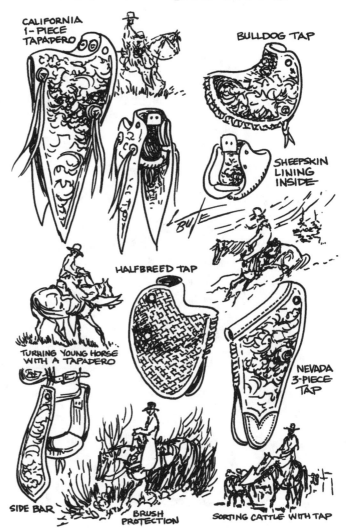

COVERED STIRRUPS

CALIFORNIA 1-PIECE TAPADERO

BULLDOG TAP

SHEEPSKIN LINING INSIDE

HALFBREED TAP

TURNING YOUNG HORSE WITH A TAPADERO

NEVADA 3-PIECE TAP

SIDE BAR

BRUSH PROTECTION

SORTING CATTLE WITH TAP

HORSE BITS—

COPPER

REGULAR SPADE

COPPER "CRICKET" ROLLER

SPOON SPADE

"SALINAS" PORT
WEST COAST FAVORITE

FAR WEST "SPADE" BITS

HORSE ROLLS WITH TONGUE-PACIFICATION AND MOIST TENDER MOUTH RESULT—

L BUTE

THE STANDARD LOW PORT BIT

GENTLE BIT USED ALL OVER THE WEST

TOM THUMB COLT BIT

INLAID COPPER STRIPS CAUSE SALIVA FLOW

KEEP MOUTH RECEPTIVE TO BIT & REIN CUES

CHEEK DESIGNS - A SAMPLING

U.S.   GRAZER   ROPER   TOM THUMB   SANTA BARBARA   LAS CRUCES   VISALIA

SNAFFLES

EGGBUTT   D-RING   LOOSE RING

AND — MANY MORE —

responds quickly to the curb that hits the roof of its mouth when the rider pulls on the reins. The most severe bit, used on the most headstrong horses, is the spade bit. It is popular with *vaqueros* and is responsible for the responsiveness of their horses. The outside of the bits range from simple rings that rest against the horse's cheeks to elaborately engraved silver works of art. Sometimes they'll match a cowboy's silver spurs.

Instead of open reins, buckaroos often use closed reins, a single rein attached on each end to the bosal. They're particularly fond of reins made out of a horsehair rope, called a *mecate*, but usually pronounced McCarty. When the horsehair alternates in colors, they're called salt-and-pepper ropes. Mecate ropes are kind of prickly, but buckaroos solve that problem by washing them in Ivory soap.

Form meets function in a cowboy's rig. Once the function is taken care of, the decoration begins. Cowboy gear is prettied up with stamping, tooling, carving, engraving, braiding, stitching, lacing, or with silver, copper, or even a touch of gold.

Cowboy Wisdom

Better the silver jewelry on the horse than on the rider.

Polishing your pants on saddle leather don't make you a rider.

It takes a lot of wet saddles to train a horse.

COW PONIES

A COWBOY WOULDN'T feel the way he does about his job and his life if it weren't for his horse. He spends more time in the saddle than he does on foot. Riding horses is what makes it all possible—and worthwhile. "The outside of a horse is good for the inside of a man," Will Rogers once said.

A cowboy on horseback feels like he owns the whole world. Four feet off the ground, the air is purer, the view is sharper. No wonder the cowboy has so often been referred to as the knight of the plains. A cowboy will tell you that riding horseback is an experience that satisfies all the senses.

Galloping through the hills on a warm spring day a cowboy feels the wind on his face, smells the wet sweet grass, sees newborn baby calves, and hears the sound of silence, except for the steady rhythm of his horse's hooves. It's all the better when the horse between his legs is a great

one with heart and a smooth gallop. "Cowboying is a hard life," admits one cowboy. "The pay's not good. There's no retirement. But I just love to ride horses."

Cowboys often refer to their horses as ponies, regardless of their size. A cow pony is a horse used for working with cattle—cutting out cows, trailing cattle, rounding up steers, roping calves. A good cow pony does the real work on a cattle ranch, so the better the horse, the better the cowboy. The relationship is not quite as romantic as the movies portray. Trigger and Silver were well-groomed sidekicks practically wedded to Roy and the Ranger. In reality, a cowboy thinks of his horse as a well-trained tool as much as a loyal partner. "I always figured that if someone offered me more for my horse than I thought he was worth, I'd sell him," said one old cowboy. But a

Working cowboys are polygamous, with as many as six horses in their string. Different horses have different temperaments and different skills. One horse might be better at cutting cattle, another might be shy of the lariat, another might excel at trailing cattle, another might be night blind. But an all-around cow pony should be a generalist.

When cowboys compare horses, they talk about hands. Horses do have four feet, but they're measured in hands, not feet. Cowboys don't carry rulers in their pockets, so if they want to measure the size of their horse, they use their hands. One hand is the width of a man's hand, a little over four inches. An average horse stands fifteen hands from the top of his withers, where his neck meets his back. A Shetland pony stands eight hands, while a shire horse used to pull wagons might stand nineteen hands.

★ A buckaroo brings home a runaway. Both horses have mecate reins, made from braided horsehair. (James Fain) ★

lot of sentimental guys would disagree. They put the old horses out to pasture and let them die natural deaths. That's why cowkids often learn to ride on Grandpa's old gelding.

Cowboys don't need to look under a horse's tail to determine its sex. They can tell from a horse's conformation and behavior whether a horse is a filly or a colt, a mare or a gelding or stallion. "I like to ride mares," insists one old Montana cowboy. "They just have more get-up-and-go." But most cowboys prefer to ride geldings (male horses that have been castrated to prevent them from becoming family men). "Geldings are much quieter than mares," insists another cowboy. "And, unlike stallions, they don't have anything else on their minds."

It's more than just male bonding. Geldings are considered to be more even-tempered than mares, and good stallions, in full possession of the family jewels, are too valuable and temperamental to ride every day. Male horses are usually castrated between one and two years of age, when the owner has had enough time to evaluate its potential ability. If they're gelded, they can stay with the mares. If they're not, they have to be kept away from the

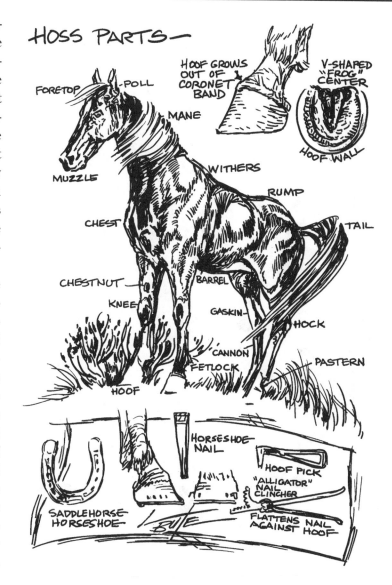

HOSS PARTS—

FORETOP
POLL
MANE
MUZZLE
WITHERS
CHEST
RUMP
TAIL
CHESTNUT
BARREL
KNEE
GASKIN
HOCK
CANNON
FETLOCK
PASTERN
HOOF

HOOF GROWS OUT OF CORONET BAND
V-SHAPED "FROG" CENTER
HOOF WALL

HORSESHOE NAIL
HOOF PICK
"ALLIGATOR" NAIL CLINCHER
FLATTENS NAIL AGAINST HOOF
SADDLEHORSE HORSESHOE

THE FAMOUS HOOLIHAN

A GOOD HORSE LOOP —

A VERSATILE LARIAT THROW —

"... I'M GOIN' TO MONTANA TO THROW THE HOOLIHAN..."
— OLD COWBOY SONG

PALM OUT AND RELEASE

WRIST TWIST

PALM IN

START

A TWIST OF THE WRIST IS SECRET OF HOOLIHAN THROW —

BUTE

mares in a separate corral. They're allowed visiting privileges in the springtime when the mares come into heat. That's when a stallion earns his keep. A good stallion can service up to 100 mares in a good season. "It's too much trouble to have a stallion around," insists one rancher who buys colts at local horse shows or pays a stud fee and has his mares bred at other ranches.

One of the first questions a dude asks when he arrives at the corral is "What's the horse's name?" In *The Culpepper Cattle Company,* the cowboy answers the greenhorn's query with, "Son, you don't name something you may have to eat." Those days are over, but cowboys still don't place much stock in naming animals. My father owns a twelve-year-old horse that everyone still refers to as "the gray mare." Traditionally it was the bronc buster who named the horses as he broke them. If a horse had any flesh marks or characteristics, it would show up in the name. Every ranch had its share of horses named Big Red, Tar Baby, Smoky, Star, Baldy. When I visited a friend's ranch and asked him to name the horses in the corral, here's the list he reeled off: Pinto, Joker, Mare, Red, Fatso, Pinhead, and Apple (short for Appaloosa).

Registered horses, those blue-blooded horses whose bloodlines can be traced back to the Mayflower or at least to the Pony Express, are a different story. Their names often incorporate the names of their sire and dam (father and mother) so that breeders can guess the bloodlines when they hear the horse's name. Town Policy, for example, was by Reb's Policy out of Camptown Girl. Eyed Be Impressive is the offspring of Mr. Impressive and Two-eyed Donna. My brother has a registered quarter horse with papers giving his name as Shy Old Dude. We call him Gus.

While cowboys pride themselves on being able to ride anything on four legs, they're particularly fond of these three breeds:

AMERICAN QUARTER HORSE

Cowboys admire thoroughbreds, those long-limbed, hot-blooded horses bred for speed, but they usually ride quarter horses. Thoroughbreds are too nervous to work with cattle, too leggy to stop short, and too delicate and thin skinned to live half wild. But they are often crossed with other breeds to produce a cow horse with "heart," something every cowboy desires in a horse. "Thoroughbreds have an extra quality other than speed," said Samuel Riddle, the owner of the legendary Man of War. "Thoroughbreds don't cry."

The American quarter horse was the first horse breed that could be called "Made in America." Called a warm-blood horse, it's a cross between a hot-blooded thoroughbred (Arabians and

Barbs) and a cold-blooded horse (usually from northern Europe). The names refer to temperament rather than temperature. (Horses' blood is all the same temperature, of course.) The name comes from the fact that they were used to run quarter-mile races. "A quarter horse is a short winded low geared race horse," scoffed one critic. Cowboys would disagree and fight to defend the horse's honor. A quarter horse's sprinting ability makes it just right for ranch work, where a horse might have to move like lightning to cut off an ornery cow. Its strength and size make it the best roping horse. And it has a lot of cow sense.

Texans can take credit for the first quarter horse with a pedigree, registered in 1940 when the American Quarter Horse Association was formed. A cross between a thoroughbred stallion and a black pony mare, the colt was named Wimpy. Despite the ignominy of his name, Wimpy started a dynasty. But he's been eclipsed by Three Bars, who sired the most respected line of quarter horses. Three Bars sired fourteen running champs and his records still stand twenty years after his death. A list of his progeny reads like the *Who's Who* of quarter horses. The sixty-four-dollar question among breeders is how do you measure the amount of Three Bars in your horse? And how much is needed to produce a winner?

Cowboy Wisdom

Horses are partners, not pets.

If a man allows you to ride his favorite horse, he's paid you the highest compliment.

Admire a big horse but saddle a small one. The biggest horses aren't the best travelers.

A horse with white hooves is more expensive than a horse with black feet.

★

ARABIAN

Known for its fiery temperament, graceful carriage, slender legs, elegant head, and wide-set eyes, the Arabian is the aristocrat of the horse world. It can trace its lineage back two thousand years to when its forebears raced across deserts with sheiks on their backs. Arab royals kept careful records of pedigrees and prized their mares as much as their money, possibly because they didn't geld their horses. A little mare could get by on little water, and her muzzle was said to be so delicate she could drink out of a teacup. Maybe that's why some cowboys insist that Arabians are afraid of water.

The first Arabians were brought to the New World by Hernando Cortés when he invaded Mexico in 1520. They were the progenitors of the mustangs, the wild horses that once ranged the West and were the staple of ranch remudas. A horse with Arabian blood is usually a solid color or dappled, seldom spotted. It can be picked out of a herd by the proud carriage of its head, its long graceful neck, high-set tail, and sculpted frame.

★ After hours the remuda runs free. (*Mark MacLeod*) ★

MORGAN

The father of the Morgan, a breed known for its athletic ability and strength, was a dark bay with black mane and tail. The stallion was owned by a Vermont singing teacher named Justin Morgan. The vocalist got the small, fine-boned colt in payment of a debt from a farmer. The little stallion, a cross between a thoroughbred and an Arabian, could outwalk, outtrot, and outrun all the other Yankee horses. He could pull a plow all day and still have some fire left in his engine to prance all the way home. Horse owners came from miles around to breed their mares with Justin Morgan's stallion. They were a mixed brood, so his offspring come in all shapes and sizes. But they all have the same compact body, round barrel, and full neck. What's more, they all have the eagerness to go. Comanche, the lone survivor of the Battle of the Big Horn, Custer's last stand, was a Morgan. Today the Morgan is considered a good utility horse. He's prized for his gentleness, intelligence, and cow sense.

COATS OF MANY COLORS

Tenderfeet often confuse horse colors with horse breeds. But despite the proliferation of horse associations that register horses, no breed can be established solely on color. You can count on the offspring of two racehorses being a fast runner. But you can't count on two palominos producing a little gold mine. It's all in the genes. Some color genes are recessive and others are dominant, and only a geneticist knows for sure.

One of the first things a horse wrangler needs to learn is the color chart for horses. If he's sent to the corral to saddle a bay, he'd better not bring back a sorrel. He just might have to ride him. Here's a guide to the fourteen most common equine colors in hopes that you won't make that mistake.

★ A foal of a different color. (*Robin Baker*) ★

1. APPALOOSA. These distinctive spotted horses were once the war ponies of the Nez Percé Indians of the Palouse country of eastern Washington and Oregon. When the Nez

Percé were defeated by the calvary, the people and the horses scattered. Today Appaloosas are quarter horses with spots— strong, sturdy, and highly prized by cowboys. There are two types of Appaloosas. The polka-dot variety is white or cream-colored and covered all over with black, brown, or auburn spots. Blanket-hip Appaloosas have solid-colored foreparts and a spotted or flecked pattern on their hips and buttocks.

2. BAY. These horses were highly prized by the Arabs, who said that any horse but a bay was unlucky unless it had white spots. Bay is a reddish brown coat of varying intensities:

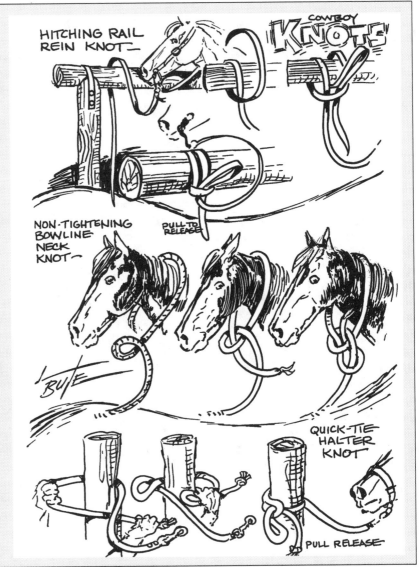

COWBOY KNOTS

HITCHING RAIL REIN KNOT

PULL TO RELEASE

NON-TIGHTENING BOWLINE NECK KNOT

BUTE

QUICK-TIE HALTER KNOT

PULL RELEASE

dark bay, mahogany bay, a blood bay, standard bay, and light bay. No matter what the first name, a bay horse should have black points—mane and tail, legs and hooves.

3. BLACK.

These are rare on the range, maybe because black horses suffer the most from the heat. Their coal black coats heat up like an oven. Horses are called black only when their coat, mane, tail, and legs are completely black. There's no doubt that black horses are beauties, but their coats tend to fade in hotter climates. Cowboys know that black horses require lots of grooming to maintain their look. And

HOSS MARKINGS

LEG MARKINGS—

SOCKS

STOCKINGS

"EQUINE FINGERPRINTS"
FACE MARKINGS

SNIP

SPOT

MARKINGS ARE USED FOR IDENTIFICATION ON REGISTRATION, BRAND AND BILL OF SALE PAPERS FOR HORSES —

STAR

STRIPE

RACE

BLAZE

BALDFACE

UNUSUAL LEG MARKINGS CALLED BOOTS

CORONET

WHITE HAIR LINE OVER TOP OF HOOF

ored. Maybe that's why buckskins are known for their endurance. A true buckskin is the color of tanned deerhide, but the shades range from yellow to gold to almost brown. The points (mane, tail, and legs) are usually black or dark brown. Buckskins often have dark dorsal stripes running from their manes to the tip of their tails.

6. CHESTNUT. This is a shade of reddish brown. Cowboys are especially fond of chestnuts, saying that they have more sense or that they are faster than other horses. The real reason may be that chestnuts have more thoroughbred blood.

7. DUN. A yellowish or gold shade, dun horses often have a different-colored mane and tails of other colors. A black dorsal strip is common. They're not what you would call pretty, but they're said to be long horses, meaning they're good for long distances.

grooming is not something that cowboys spend a lot of time on.

4. BROWN. These horses have very durable hides but, like black horses, they're prone to sunburn, the cowboy term for bleaching out. Many horses that look brown are actually bays or chestnuts. True browns are seal-skin colored.

5. BUCKSKIN. Some cowboys believe that the first horses were buckskin col-

8. GRAY. A gray horse is an optical illusion. Its skin is black and its hair is white, or salt-and-pepper. A dappled gray is a mottled gray, with black hairs around the white flecks. When they're young, gray horses are dark. But just like old cowboys, they turn silver or white as they get older.

9. GRULLA.

Cowboys say a grulla is mouse-colored. Grullas are bluish gray and said to be the toughest horses in the West.

10. PAINT.

Paint horses have been called many names over the years—pintos, paints, piebalds, skewbalds. The splashy mounts were always popular with Indians but many cowboys didn't like paint horses. "All a paint horse is worth is to ride him down the road," said one cowboy. They were strong and hardy, but they never got very big. Paints started to get some respect in the 1960s when the Paint Horse Association was formed. Paint horses come in many colors and patterns. Piebalds are black and white,

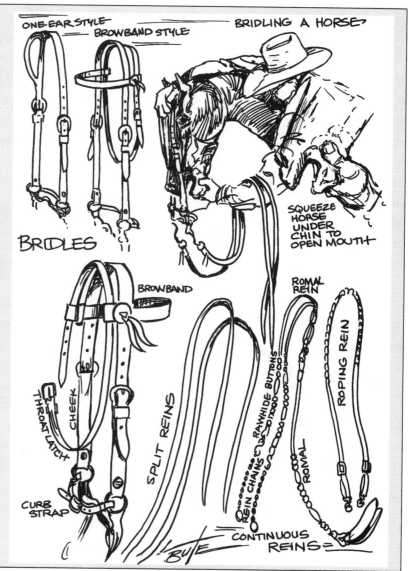

ONE-EAR STYLE
BROWBAND STYLE
BRIDLING A HORSE?
BRIDLES
SQUEEZE HORSE UNDER CHIN TO OPEN MOUTH
BROWBAND
THROAT LATCH
CHEEK
SPLIT REINS
RAWHIDE BUTTONS
REIN CHAINS
ROMAL REIN
ROMAL
ROPING REIN
CURB STRAP
BUIE
CONTINUOUS REINS

while skewbalds are white with chestnut, brown, or yellow. A paint with no white over his back is called an overo. If he has four white feet and abnormal face markings, he's a tobiano. Those are the general rules, but Mother Nature doesn't play by the rules. But you won't go wrong if you call it a paint.

11. PALOMINO. This golden beauty is a favorite mount of movie stars and parade riders. Breeders say that a true palomino is a horse the color of a newly minted U.S. gold coin with mane and tail a natural white. Palominos originated in California, naturally, the land of summer blondes. You have to care how you look to ride a palomino. Their amber hooves tend to be brittle, their hides are sensitive, and they prefer to stay out of the sun. Some riders can handle the restrictions and grooming that keep these golden beauties gleaming. Not many cowboys, though.

12. ROAN. Think of a roan as a haze of white hair clouding the color of the horse's hide. Roans vary in shade according to their underlying skin color. Blue roans have black skin, while red roans have chestnut skin. One of the most famous roans is the outlaw immortalized in the old cowboy song, "The Strawberry Roan."

13. SORREL. This is a reddish amber color. A sorrel horse can't camouflage its draft-horse roots. True sorrels should have manes and tails the same color as their coat. Lighter sorrels have flaxen manes and tails. All sorrels tend to get darker from the ground up. From the knees down the color lightens at least a shade. Cowboys know they have tender hides and take extra care when bridling and saddling to prevent chafing.

14. WHITE. You've no doubt seen a white horse, but you'll never see a white colt. That's because a colt is born with a dark coat that later turns white. Most cowboys will shun a chalk white horse, fearing that it's a product of too much inbreeding.

HORSE SENSE

★ A cowboy prides himself on being able to ride anything on four feet. (*Stephen Collector*) ★

THERE'S AN OLD song that says "Don't call him a cowboy until you've seen him ride." A cowboy and his horse ride in harmony, the cowboy's body relaxed, synchronized with the horse's gait. Ray Hunt, one of the gurus of the horse-training world, describes it this way: "In your own mind, you have to have a picture of what you want from the horse, but you are the leader and you can ask him to follow you, just like dancing. It's a rhythm, a harmony—you want your body and his body to become one."

A cowboy can do on horseback what most people have a problem doing on foot, opening a gate, for instance. On the range, a man on foot is no

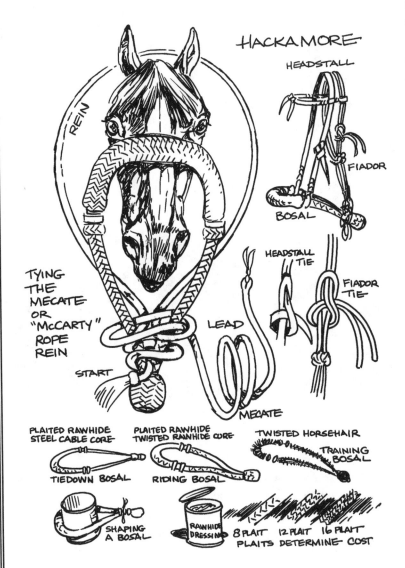

HACKAMORE

HEADSTALL

REIN

FIADOR

BOSAL

HEADSTALL TIE

FIADOR TIE

TYING THE MECATE OR "McCARTY" ROPE REIN

START

LEAD

MECATE

PLAITED RAWHIDE STEEL CABLE CORE

TIEDOWN BOSAL

PLAITED RAWHIDE TWISTED RAWHIDE CORE

RIDING BOSAL

TWISTED HORSEHAIR

TRAINING BOSAL

SHAPING A BOSAL

RAWHIDE DRESSING

8 PLAIT   12 PLAIT   16 PLAIT
PLAITS DETERMINE COST

man at all. It's almost like an unwritten code of the West.

Eastern riders pride themselves on formal riding style; cowboys pride themselves on being able to stick to anything on four legs (and then ride it with ease). Just keeping a leg on each side of a colt is all that matters in real life. When a horse bucks, the rider doesn't have time to think about technique—he's too busy trying to stay on or picking out a soft place to land. That's why cowboys view classic dressage as esoteric training that has no application to practical everyday riding. When cutting cattle or roping steers, there's no place for slow, unnatural gaits.

Wranglers used to say, "There ain't a horse that can't be rode. And there ain't a man that can't be thrown." If a horse is going to explode—start to buck—it'll do it within the first few minutes.

Bronc busters once relied on dominance. A tough cowboy would ride an old outlaw into submission. Those ideas are yesterday's news. Today cowboys listen to the gospel according to Tom Dorrance, known far and wide as the horse's lawyer. No matter what the problem, Dorrance always defends the horse. Dorrance developed a method of starting horses, as opposed to breaking horses; it could be called "Zen and the Art of Horse Training." It relies on unity, harmony, and most of all, a round corral (no corners where a horse can hide).

Today cowboys start colts when they are about two years old. The horse is let out to move around the corral at will until it finds a place where it feels comfortable. Everything is done to prevent a horse from buck-

★

Cowboy Wisdom

Never approach a horse in anger. You've got to control your temper before you can control your horse.

★

ing. Bucking is a bad habit that's hard to break. "There's a real art to breaking colts," admits one cowboy. "Try to make them your friend and keep them that way, you won't have as many battles. Be calm and casual with your horses and they'll be that way with you."

Once the horse feels comfortable on this new turf, he's roped—on the foot, the buttocks, the hips, to get used to the feel of the rope and prepare it for saddling. "Work both sides of the horse," advises Hunt, although most horses are later trained to be mounted from the left side. Once the horse is used to the rope, he's introduced to the halter and then the saddle. When Hunt takes his first ride on a horse, he does so without a halter or bridle. He uses a coiled rope to direct the horse to

★ Buckaroos are known for their horse sense.
(*Robin Barker*) ★

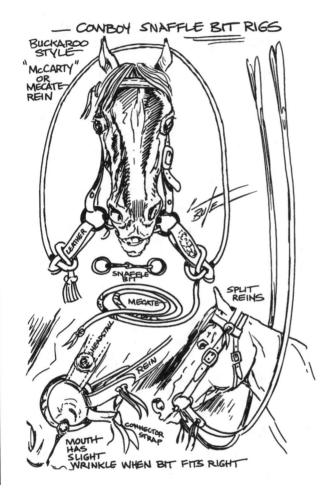

— COWBOY SNAFFLE BIT RIGS

BUCKAROO STYLE

"McCARTY" OR MECATE REIN

LEATHER

SNAFFLE BIT

MECATE

SPLIT REINS

HEADSTALL

REIN

CONNECTOR STRAP

MOUTH HAS SLIGHT WRINKLE WHEN BIT FITS RIGHT

frequent handling of many horses. To become a great horseman, a cowboy has to put the book down, climb off the top rail, and get into the corral with the horse. All the gurus of the horse world—Dorrance, Hunt, Lyons, Buster Welch—say that most of what they learned about horsemanship came from the horse.

"It's humbling to realize that we aren't teaching a horse to do anything he doesn't already know," says John Mike Downey, an accomplished horse trainer in Butte, Montana. "Even an unschooled horse can stop, turn, spin, back up, jump, and lay down. It's up to us to learn how to communicate to him to do these things on command."

Cowboys may not speak French or German, but they can communicate in the horse's language. For example, if a cowboy wants to tell his horse that he's doing a good job, he won't pat him or slap him on the back, the way football players do after a player has scored a touchdown. That only startles a horse. Equine affection is shown by mutual nuzzling of back and manes. A horse's first experience with affection was when he came into the world and his mother licked him. Mother knows best, so cowboys use their hands to lavish affection and praise

where he wants it to go, by moving it from one side of his neck to the other.

At least 95 percent of horse sense comes from

Cowboy Wisdom

Horses are only afraid of two things—things that move and things that don't.

If your horse will mind you in the barn, he'll mind you in the field.

Good riding is done more with your head than with the seat of your pants.

Only fools or gamblers walk behind a strange horse.

★

You can't tell a horse's gait until he's broke.

★ Cowboy guru Ray Hunt practices what he preaches: harmony with horses. (*Julie Chase*) ★

on their horses. Trainer John Lyons says: "The best tool in the barn is at the end of your arm."

Just by being near a horse, you are sending it signals. A horse can sense if a rider is scared or if he doesn't like him. Horses can recognize their usual rider by how he handles, saddles, or touches the horse. They recognize a cowboy's smell, shape, size, even the size of his hat. If a cowboy wears a baseball hat when he's training a young horse and one day shows up in a big cowboy hat, the horse will be confused and a little skittish.

By nature, horses are herd animals and show their affection to other members of their band. Probably the biggest compliment a horse can pay his owner is when the horse is in the corral or pasture with his buddies and he chooses to come over to his owner. It's a dead giveaway that the cowboy has taken the time and care to understand and respect his horse. And the horse has transferred his loyalty to his owner or rider. Once the bond is established, the horse will try his darndest to follow commands. This attachment is part of what makes a cowboy love his job.

GETTING TO KNOW A HORSE

There are a few tricks to getting acquainted with a new horse. Let him smell you, rub his neck and back, scratch his face, talk to him, assure him that you're not going to hurt him. A smart cowboy watches the gauges on a horse just like a race car driver watches the gauges on a car. He can tell what's on a horse's mind by watching the horse's eyes and ears. They'll show where his attention is focused and what's his mood.

• Ears forward means that he's paying attention to what's going on around him.

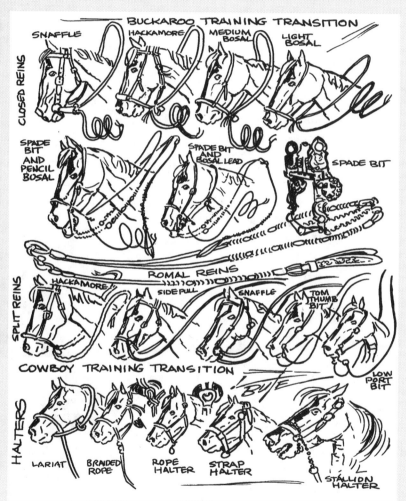

BUCKAROO TRAINING TRANSITION

SNAFFLE   HACKAMORE   MEDIUM BOSAL   LIGHT BOSAL

CLOSED REINS

SPADE BIT AND PENCIL BOSAL   SPADE BIT AND BOSAL LEAD   SPADE BIT

ROMAL REINS

SPLIT REINS

HACKAMORE   SIDE PULL   SNAFFLE   TOM THUMB BIT   LOW PORT BIT

COWBOY TRAINING TRANSITION

HALTERS

LARIAT   BRAIDED ROPE   ROPE HALTER   STRAP HALTER   STALLION HALTER

- Ears relaxed means that you can relax. The horse trusts you, is feeling self-confident and willing to do what's asked of him.
- Ears drooping to the side means that he's not paying attention to anything in particular, he's daydreaming, or even asleep. Don't touch him without first getting his attention. You might startle him.
- Ears pointing back shows anger or fear.
- Ears pinned back against his neck is the run-for-cover sign. Pay attention, because an angry horse might bite, strike, or kick. A famous painting by Charles M. Russell depicts a horse with his ears pinned back. Russell summed it all up when he captioned the work: "When horses talk war, there is no chance for peace."

COWBOYS DON'T GROOM

Cow ponies are fairly self-sufficient. They're never blanketed or brought into the barn when it's cold outside. That's why they grow extra hair in winter.

Stable horses may get lots of grooming, but most cow horses are strangers to curry combs and bristle brushes. They typically groom themselves by rolling in the dirt. After shaking themselves off, they shine as if they'd been rubbed and waxed.

★ Cowboys don't groom but they do know how to shoe horses. (*James Fain*) ★

BEYOND THE TROT

Even though quarter horses were bred for their speed, no self-respecting cowboy would gallop his horse out of the corral. Just like any other athlete, horses need time to warm up. A good cowboy trains his horse to shift gears on command. A horse has five speeds or gaits: walk, trot, lope, gallop, run.

★ Nothing beats a fast ride in the springtime. (*Appaloosa Horse Club*) ★

A **WALK** is the horse's slowest gait because he always has two feet on the ground. A brisk walk is one of the horse's best and smoothest gaits. A good horse shouldn't dawdle but should maintain an energetic ground-eating walk. Many of the best cow horses can manage a race walk.

The **TROT** is second gear on a horse. The horse lifts his front and back feet on opposite sides at the same time. A rapid-fire trot can loosen all the teeth in your mouth. A trot is the cowboy's least favorite gait because he rides close to the saddle. If they have to trot, cowboys stand up in their stirrups to cushion the ride. Old-timers call this stance the "North Dakota trot" or the "Montana shag." It guarantees a smoother ride, but the rider's legs will give out after a short distance. That's why cowboys have learned to post when they trot. A post trot is a combination of sitting and standing in the stirrups. This is one time when a cowboy can hold the saddle horn. A rider reacts to the horse's motion and his body bobs up and down in perfect rhythm with his horse. A post trot can be kept up for fairly long distances.

A **GALLOP** is a smooth succession of leaps. A **LOPE** is a slow gallop and a **RUN** is a fast gallop. A good cow horse can lope for miles and the rider can relax and enjoy the smooth ride. On the larger ranches, good lope horses are in such great demand that they're assigned on the basis of seniority. The veteran cowboys get first pick. When buying a horse of his own, a cowboy looks for a horse with a smooth slow gallop and a fast walk. A fast horse is sometimes needed but smoothness usually wins out over speed.

The way a horse comes to a stop is as important as the way he gallops. A jolting, rough stop that practically catapults the rider across the field does not endear the horse to the rider. Even if he doesn't lose his seat, he's sure to lose his temper and cuss the horse. Every cowboy would like his horse to master a smooth, sliding stop.

★ All in a day's ride. (*Robin Barker*) ★

★

Cowboy Wisdom

Your stirrups are the right length if you can stand up in the stirrups and your rear end clears the saddle.

★

CRITTERS

WHEN A COWBOY says "critter," he means cow—critter is short for creature. When cowboys talk about cows, they mean it generically, boys and girls. Calves are babies, heifers are young cows, steers are neutered boy cows, and bulls are the daddy of them all. How many cows can one bull handle? That's a question that cowboys have been trying to figure out for years. Some breeders brag that their bulls can handle fifty cows. Most ranches try to have extra bulls on hand in case one "breaks down" during mating season, but that's expensive. The standard ratio is somewhere between 1:20 and 1:30. But in rough country where bulls have to go out and look for the cows, the ratio is more like 1:12.

You can't talk about cowboys unless you talk about cows. They're *cow*boys, after all, not horseboys. A cowboy can just look at a cow and tell if she's healthy. Her coat will tell him if she's on good feed. Her eyes will tell if she's in some kind of trouble. A cowboy can look at a heifer and tell when she's going to spill her first calf. One glance at a calf will tell if it's sucked today or if it's lost its mother.

Some people don't forget a face. Well, good cowboys never forget a cow. They think of them as individuals and remember details about cows. Like, that old cow with the twisted horns likes to hide in the willows. Or that cow with the white neck, number 99, will lead the herd. Or that butterscotch cow will charge a horse.

A cowboy's job is to tend the cows. The cows in turn tend the calves. Each cow knows her calf. By eating the calf's afterbirth, she knows her little one's odor, and she can pick her baby out of a herd of hundreds. Sometimes cowboys have to

BOVINE GENEALOGY—
LONGHORN

!BUTE

SHORTHORN

HEREFORD

BRAHAMA

SIMMENTAL

BLACK BALDY

ANGUS

THE RESULT—   A BALD-FACED LIE

help nature a bit. Say a cow loses her calf and another has twins. Rather than letting two calves suck off one mother cow, they'll take the dead calf's hide and tie it over one of the twins. Soon that lonely mother cow will be nursing one of the twins.

Cows are constantly on a cowboy's mind, morning, noon, and night. He worries about when to put the bulls in with the cows. When will the heifers calve? When to move cattle to the hills? He's constantly culling his herd to improve its quality. If a heifer doesn't breed, she's sold in the fall. If a cow gets foot rot, she's sent down the road. If a cow calves late, she might not be given a second chance. Raising cattle is a lot like gambling, so cowboys cut their losses early and often.

Counting cows is the way a rancher counts his money. He gets one big paycheck a year—when he ships the calves in the fall. Ranchers count on cows having a calf a year for nine years. When cowboys count cows, they're talking about mother cows, not calves. A cow is considered a mother-calf unit. There's a trick to counting up a pasture full of cows. You don't count cows one at a time—it would take all day. My grandfather had a way of counting them by fives, with a flick of his wrist.

Anyone who grew up on TV Westerns knows that the early-day Texas ranchers raised long-horns. By the end of the Civil War, Texas was home to some six million longhorns. The breed was tough and self-sufficient. They could go long distances without water, and if they were properly handled on trail drives, they could actually gain weight on the long trip north to the railroads. But the breed did not produce tender flavorful meat or much of it.

When barbed wire and windmills opened up the West to ranching, cattlemen began to look for breeds that were more efficient meat producers. British breeds were not as self-sufficient as their longhorned cousins, but they gained more weight, which translated into bigger bucks for

★ A cowboy cuts out the babies at branding time. (*James Fain*) ★

ranchers. By nature, these European breeds were more docile and easier to handle. And their short horns reduced a cowboy's chances of being gored by a steer's horn. By 1927 Texas longhorns were close to extinction. The federal government allocated $3,000 to purchase and preserve a herd of Texas longhorns.

Surprisingly, longhorns are experiencing somewhat of a comeback. Many ranchers have come to believe that a longhorn is the bull of choice with a virgin heifer. The crossbred calf has a smaller head, making it easier for the first-time mother to deliver the calf.

Breeding great cattle sounds simple: All you have to do is breed the best bulls with the best cows. But breeding great cattle isn't easy. Fences fall down, bulls break down, cows go dry. Despite the use of artifical insemination, genetics, and high technology, cattle breeding is an inexact science that relies on good stock, good weather, and good luck.

There are dozens of breeds of beef cattle, each with its own strengths, weaknesses, and national association. Each organization registers cattle and keeps records of bloodlines, tracking the progeny of champion bulls. Serious breeders can name the bulls of choice the way sport fans can name World Series players. Here's a short guide to the standard cattle breeds and what real cowboys think of them.

- **Angus**. These muscular black cows that have their roots in Scotland are popular on northern ranges. Their dark skin protects them from sunburn (something that can happen to a cow's nipples on a sunny winter day when there's snow on the ground).
- **Beefmaster**. This crossbreed, a mixture of Hereford, shorthorn, and Brahman, was first produced at the Lasater Ranch in Colorado.
- **Brahman**. This humped breed is descended from zebu cattle of India. Cattleman Shanghai Pierce imported them into Texas in the 1880s because they were resistant to tick fever. Tough and fierce, the Brahman is said to be the only cow that can stage a stampede by herself. Brahman bulls are often used as rodeo stock.

Cowboy Wisdom

Never ask a rancher the size of his herd or the number of acres he owns.

Nobody but cattle know why they stampede and they ain't talking.

★

- **Belgian Blue**. This big, beefy Belgian breed is distinctive because of its muscular rump and shoulders. Purebreds looks like bloated bovine bodybuilders. They're mostly used for crossbreeding.
- **Brangus**. This crossbreed is ⅜ Brahman and ⅝ Angus.
- **Charolais**. This French breed is known for its king-size cream-colored cattle. They're often used in crossbreeding to ensure bigger, fatter calves at sale time.
- **Corriente**. An up-and-comer, this breed was developed in Mexico from cattle brought from Spain in the seventeenth century. It's the most popular breed of cattle for team roping and steer wrestling. They are small, strong, and quick, and their prominent horns making them good targets for ropers.
- **Galloway**. This furry breed has two coats of hair. It sheds its outer coat in hot weather. Most Galloways are brown, black, or tan. One variety, the Belted Galloway, is called the Oreo Cookie cow because of its chocolate brown head and tail sections and wide white belt in the middle.
- **Hereford**. Classic cattle on the northern ranges, Herefords have white faces and red bodies. They're good meat producers, but prone to eye ailments.
- **Longhorn**. America's first cattle, long-horns were brought to Mexico by Spanish settlers in the 1500s. Rangy fierce animals with horns that spread up to six feet, they crossed the Rio Grande and spread in the southwest. They roamed as far north as the Red River separating Texas and Oklahoma. Tough and self-sufficient, longhorns could go a long way without water. But the breed was eclipsed by better meat producers. Dehorning has eliminated the problem of the swordlike horns, and the breed is experiencing something of a comeback.
- **Santa Gertrudis**. The first breed developed in the western hemisphere. The King Ranch of Texas produced this cherry red crossbreed with its loose hide, a mixture of Brahman, short-horn, and longhorn. Santa Gertrudis cows are known as protective mothers that help each other out. In the bovine version of babysitting, one cow will tend all the calves while the other mothers graze.
- **Shorthorn**. This British breed was popular with early colonists because of its versatility. Shorthorns provide beef and milk and they were also used as draft animals. They're still known for their easy disposition and good meat production.
- **Simmental**. This breed has its origins in Switzerland. Once used as draft animals, they're known for their size, longevity, and strong feet and legs. The original European purebreds were red-

and-white or yellow-and-white and were known for their dairy prowess. Today Simmentals can range from almost solid black to patchy colors to almost white and are raised for beef. They can be picked out of the herd by their solid size, low-set ears, large heads, and loose folds around their dewlaps.

Cowboy Wisdom

A cow's job is to have a calf as often as possible. A cowboy's job is to see that the calf gets to market.

BISON PRESERVES

The old cowboys used to yearn for a home where the buffalo roam. But these days that's a lot of wishful thinking. In 1830, the year that buffalo hunts began in earnest, there were some 40 million buffalo at home on the range. Fifty years later only a few stragglers remained. Hunters often killed 250 in a day and many said that they killed 3,000 in a year. They left the carcasses to rot in the sun, and carried the hides, robes, and tongues back to trading posts. By the turn of the century, massive hunts, like the famous Red River Hunt, had turned the bison into an endangered species, with fewer than 300 animals in the wild.

In 1894 Congress finally sat up, took notice, and took action to save the species. It passed an act making buffalo hunting in Yellowstone National Park, one of the last natural havens for bison, illegal. Fortunately a few wise men, notably Charles Goodnight in Texas, the Pablo and Allard families in Montana, and Buffalo Bill Cody were raising small captive herds. Money was later appropriated to buy twenty-one bison to beef up the herd in Yellowstone Park.

Today there are four national bison ranges where buffalo live nearly as their ancestors did. On the Wichita Mountains Refuge in southwestern Oklahoma, a herd of 900 range over one of the finest pastures in the country. Just under 400 live on the Moiese Range in the Flathead Valley of Montana. Northern Nebraska is home to a herd of 200 on the Fort Niobrara Range. And a small herd of 20 live on the Sullys Hill Range of northwestern North Dakota.

Besides the refuges, bison are protected on a number of national parks, including Yellowstone, Wind Cave, Grand Teton, Theodore Roosevelt National Memorial Park, and Badlands National Monument. In fact, the Yellowstone herd has grown so large, over 800 at last count, that the state of Montana tried to organize buffalo hunts just north of the park, much to the dismay of environmentalists. Public outcry against the slaughters finally forced the Fish and Game Department to deep-six plans for more hunts.

Bison also made the front page news when Ted Turner bought the huge Flying D Ranch near Bozeman, Montana, and announced that he was selling off the cattle and switching to buffalo. His neighbors practically rose in arms, fearing an outbreak of brucellosis, a disease spread by buffalo that causes cows to abort their calves. To keep the bison in their place, the neighbors have all strengthened their fences.

Over the years, many enterprising cattlemen have looked at the enormous size and hardiness of buffalo and gotten to thinking. What if I crossed a buffalo with a cow? Some did and the cross was known as a cattalo. It was big, it was hardy. Only one problem. The hybrid couldn't reproduce.

But the bison are doing just fine these days. Biologists estimate that today there are more than 10,000 buffalo at home on the range on public lands.

HOME ON THE RANCH

COWBOYS LIVE AND work on ranches, and they bristle when dudes call them farms. A patch of farmland, which is plowed, planted, and harvested, is called a field. A patch of ranchland, which is not cultivated, is called a pasture or range. Farmers grow crops in their fields. Ranchers raise livestock in their pastures.

Ranches tend to be huge, especially in the eyes of cityfolk. But in many places it takes at least 100 acres to support one cow and several thousand acres to support a family. A cowman would consider a 5,000-acre ranch to be a small ranch; a 10,000-acre ranch to be a nice family ranch; a 25,000-acre ranch to be a big ranch; and anything over 50,000 acres to be heaven on earth. The daddy of them all, King Ranch in Texas, covers more than a million acres. But don't make the mistake of asking a rancher the size of his place—or the size of his herd. That's for him to know and the tax man to find out.

Ranchers are notoriously tight-lipped when it comes to land and cattle. My father didn't know the boundaries of Bopa's ranch until two or three years after he had married my mother. It was probably another five years before he knew how many acres Bopa owned. Despite all the secrecy, everyone knows how well a rancher is doing. All you have to do is look in his fields and count his cows or check out his hay crop.

Record-keeping is as much a part of ranch life as roping and riding. Some high-tech ranchers keep track of every cow's production on the ranch computer. Others are more the back-of-an-old-envelope type of cowman. Regardless, they know the number of cows and calves they're raising, and they know what a penny more a pound

★ The ranch's front door to the outside world. (*Stephen Collector*) ★

will do to their bank accounts. Ranchers joke that they are the bankers' unwilling partners. They live on credit until they can pay off their debts when the cattle and crops are sold in the fall. They keep up with the price of commodities the way brokers watch the stock market. "It's a gamble no matter what you're raising," Bopa always said.

Many ranch families are balance-sheet millionaires, but you won't find them living high on the hog. "Ranching is the poorest return on investment that I can think of," says one North Dakota rancher. "Someone will spend one million on a ranch and they're lucky if they get a return in the single digits," points out a Montana cowboy. "Nobody can be a cat-

★

Cowboy Wisdom

Never work for a man with electricity in his barn—you'll be up all night.

★

tle baron anymore," says a Nebraska rancher. "We're lucky if we're baron*ets*."

Regardless of net worth, cowboys have long memories. They still refer to places by the original owners, as in, Peters lives on the old Kountz place or Temple lives on the old Lewis place. Even on their own ranch they refer to certain sections as the Jones place or the Smith place, the names of homesteaders who arrived first, failed fast, and packed up their bags and moved to town.

Going to town is a big deal in cattle country. For one thing, there's always work to be done. And for another, it's a long, bumpy drive. "When you go get groceries, you better be sure that you've got everything on your list," says one cowgirl, who drives

★ Sitting for a family portrait. (*Julie Chase*) ★

GOING THROUGH A BARBED WIRE FENCE

OPENING A WIRE GATE

PULLING A WIRE GATE MAY REQUIRE LEVERAGE

A COW COUNTRY LATCH

RANGELAND FENCE GATES

COWBOY MANNERS – RIDERS FACE GATE HOLDING OFF RIDER'S HORSE WHILE HE CLOSES A WIRE GATE.

half an hour over a dirt road to ranch headquarters and then an hour on a two-lane highway to get to town. When they do shop, they buy in bulk—cases of juice, sacks of potatoes, cartons of paper towels, whole boxes of canned goods. There's no running to town for a dozen eggs or a gallon of milk. Besides, they get milk from the ranch's dairy cow, milked by the kids or the hired hand. Eggs come courtesy of the ranch henhouse, where the kids are taught at an early age to help mom or grandma get the eggs. Pizza delivery and fast-food chains are considered exotic.

When cowboys talk of the home ranch, they mean the ranch's headquarters. Some bachelor cowboys still live in bunkhouses, but most live in small houses or trailers with their families. Most ranches have a shop for repairing machinery, a tack room for stor-

HORSEHAIR

WESTERNERS LOVE PLAITED HORSEHAIR BELTS AND HATBANDS

PLAITING HORSEHAIR

SHOOFLY

SHOOFLY KEEPS FLIES AWAY FROM HORSE

ANTIQUE HORSEHAIR CINCHA

TWISTING HORSEHAIR

22 FOOT MANEHAIR MECATE

MANEHAIR IS SOFT

FOR HACKAMORE & SNAFFLE BIT REINS

TAIL HAIR IS STIFF

BUTE

ing saddles and bridles, a barn for housing sick animals (cows do not live in barns on ranches), and a huge gasoline tank. Besides their monthly pay, some cowboys are allowed as much gas as they can use. They use a lot.

Cowboys drive up to the ranch house, where the owner or ranch foreman lives, and park in the barnyard. Their arrival is announced by the yips and yaps of the dogs who keep up their chorus until the owner comes to the door. There's no welcome sign written on the door mats. But that would be an overstatement. Friends, neighbors, and strangers are always welcome at the ranch.

Everyone enters the house though the kitchen door. Ranch houses do have front doors but no one uses them. Who wants to track manure on the living room rug? Only company uses the front door and even they usually traipse through the kitchen. My grandfather's living room door was so infrequently used that only a piano mover could have pushed it open.

When they come home for dinner, cowboys make a pit stop in the mud room to hang up their jackets and take off their boots. This takes a few minutes as they take turns struggling with the boot-jack.

Breakfast, which can run several courses, is served at dawn. A sturdy cowboy often fuels up at breakfast and doesn't eat again until supper. If the cowboys are working close to the house, the main meal, called dinner, is served in the middle of the day. The evening meal, called supper, is a casual affair because the cowboys might not make it home before midnight if they're calving or haying.

Cowboy Wisdom

A smart cowman is one with oil derricks on his land for cows to scratch against.

If you're in this business to make money, you better have your head examined.

★

When there's work to do, cowboys work until it's finished. Watches aren't worn, because no one is watching the clock. Cowboys work twelve hours a day, seven days a week, fifty-two weeks a year. Saturday is just another work day except that the kids get to participate.

Cowboys never sleep until the cows come home. They get up with the sun and work until the sun goes down. Late risers are accused of burning daylight. The rule is broken in winter when they get up in the dark and work until after dark.

The hired hands eat with the ranch family. That's one reason why meals at the ranch aren't quality family time. Private issues can't be discussed if outsiders are present. Chuck-wagon etiquette still prevails. Cowboys tend to sit down, serve themselves a big plate of food, eat, and ride off. One young bride complained that by the time she sat down, her cowboy groom had already eaten and was washing his plate in the sink.

Cowboys don't take vacations. Asking a neighbor to feed the cat is one thing. Asking a neighbor to keep an eye on a whole herd is quite another. They make do with long weekends, not two-week vacations at the beach. I've known more than one cowboy to change his mind about going on vacation as he walked out to the car. They were just convinced that their places would fall apart if they left.

Cowboy Wisdom

Cow skulls should be hung above the outside

door, not over the fireplace. Today's skull was

yesterday's bug banquet.

★

★ Ranch rules don't allow
the dog in the house, so it
beds down in the hay.
(*Mark MacLeod*) ★

THE RANCH HIERARCHY

★ Noon break. (*Vicki Anderson Shampeny*) ★

Every group has its own pecking order. Here's a guide to the cowboy totem pole:

1. At the top is the **RANCH OWNER,** once an individual, now just as likely to be a corporation.

2. If the ranch has an absentee owner, he employs a **GENERAL MANAGER** to fill his boots. He's more of a numbers cruncher than a cowpuncher.

3. Sometimes called the straw boss, the **RANCH FOREMAN** has all the responsibility and some of the authority. A one-minute manager, he can hire and fire the hands. And he can buy and sell the cattle.

4. The **COW BOSS** is in charge of the ranch's cattle operation and the day-to-day care of the herds. He gives the cowboys their daily riding orders.

5. **COOK**. Ranchers know that good food helps keep the cowboys around. Sometimes the foreman's wife cooks for the cowboys. On big ranches, a retired cowboy, who knows what cowboys like, slings the hash.

6. **COWBOYS**. On smaller ranches, where the ranch family does much of the cowboying, they refer to nonfamily cowboys as hired hands. Besides cowboying, these cowboys are expected to be all-around hands, able to shoe horses, mend fence, and fix machinery.

7. **HORSE WRANGLER**. On dude ranches or large ranches with huge remudas, strings of horses, an apprentice cowboy is in charge of the horses. He's expected to know all the horses by name and sight, round them up in the morning, and collect them at the end of the day.

8. **SEASONAL HELP** is at the bottom of the heap. Up north, ranchers hire high school kids to help during haying season. It's not as romantic as it sounds; they spend the days putting up hay instead of punching cattle. Down south, ranchers hire extra hands, or waddies, to help with the twice-a-year cattle roundups. When the roundup ends, the waddies hit the trail.

RANCH WOMEN

THERE ARE A lot more cowgirls today than there ever were in the days of the wild and woolly West. That's because there are a lot more women in the West. Cowgirls today come in many variations—rancher's daughter, cowboy's sweetheart, cowman's wife, hired hand, horse trainer, even cow boss or foreman.

Ranch women don't go from the cradle to the saddle. On most family ranches they can choose whether they want to work inside or outside, but they have to work. On smaller places, the whole family cowboys. On big spreads, the women might work as teachers or nurses during the week and cowgirl on weekends. If she's really gung-ho, a cowgirl who's honed her skills during the week might barrel race on weekends.

In early Westerns women are usually depicted as unhappy or fearful. Nothing could be farther from the truth. Western women were—and are—strong and independent. In *Daughter of the Earth*, Agnes Smedley wrote that the West "was a land where women were strong." Eastern women were brought up to be ladies and stayed in the house. When they rode horseback, they used a sidesaddle, a contraption designed by a misogynist to restrict their movement and keep them demure. Ranch women would have nothing to do with "riding like a lady"; they hiked up their skirts and rode the natural way—like a man.

It doesn't take brute strength to ride a horse and round up cattle, so cowgirls are accepted at the corral. The rule of the corral is that each rider saddles his own horse. (A cowboy doesn't want anyone to think that he's waiting on his woman.) If a cowgirl can saddle a horse, she can ride for the brand.

★ Raised on a Wyoming ranch, this cowgirl is a ranch foreman.
(Stephen Collector) ★

Cowboys respect their women. It probably grew out of the reality of the frontier: There were few women around. If something is scarce, you value it more. Little surprise that it was a cowboy state—Wyoming —that first gave women the right to vote. Its neighbor Montana sent the first woman to Congress. And Arizona sent the first woman—a rancher's daughter—to the Supreme Court.

Western women are doers. The Cowbelles are cattle country's equivalent of the Junior League. Besides organizing social events like saddle rides or beef cookoffs, they raise money for community needs like a new fire truck for the volunteer fire department or a new ambulance for the country hospital.

If she yearns for movie theaters and department stores, a woman is not going to be happy living in cow country. But there are lots of advantages to living on a ranch. Cowgirls don't have to work out after work to stay in shape. They have tight buns and thighs from hugging the back of a horse, their backs are strong from pitching

---

★

Cowgirl Wisdom

You can scratch a cowboy out of your brand book, but not out of your heart.

★

Love a horse before you fall in love with a man.

★

---

hay, and their arms are taut from milking cows.

Cowgirls don't worry about keeping up with the neighbors (if only they had close neighbors).

Cowgirls don't have to worry about how they look during the week (who's looking?).

Cowgirls don't spend a lot of money on makeup for that natural glow. Her usual makeup mirror is the rearview mirror of the truck. Lipstick and mascara are often applied on the way to town.

Cowgirls were not born to shop. If they shop till they drop, it's because they've driven an hour to town and stocked up on feed, seed, salt, and a month's supply of groceries. When they do hit a big city, they cram a year's worth of shopping into an afternoon.

Cowgirls have plenty of personal space. When the wagon pulls out for spring roundup they might not see their husbands for two or three weeks. Wives say that the twice-a-year sabbatical does wonders for their relationship.

Cowgirls don't have to worry about their own safety. A city girl worries about taking a walk by herself in the park. A cowgirl can saddle up and ride alone to her heart's content without worrying about encountering a thug around the next bend. She can enjoy the solitude, listen to the song of the wind, and smell the sage brush.

Cowgirl Wisdom

Even when a man holds the reins,

a woman has to be able to take

them away in a runaway.

★

★ These California cowgirls sport matching chaps and braided stampede strings with horsehair tassels. (*Julie Chase*) ★

SPRING ROUNDUP

THE BUSINESS OF ranching is grass. Cows eat the grass that grows on the land that's mortgaged to the bank to pay for more grassland. If there's plenty of rain and sunshine, the grass will be a bovine banquet. If the sky is stingy with moisture, the grass won't feed a gopher. That's why ranchers keep one eye on the horizon and the other on their bank account.

Cowboys spend late winter and early spring playing midwife to cows. Once the last calf has dropped and made its first steps on wobbly legs, it's time to think about spring roundup. In the Southwest, where cattle are pretty much on their own, spring roundup means what it sounds like. Cowboys saddle up and spend days, even weeks, rounding up the cattle and bringing them down from the hills. Up north, where cows winter close to the home ranch, roundup often doesn't amount to much more than opening the gates and herding the cattle to the branding corral.

Branding. Just the word is music to the ears of winter-weary cowboys. It's pure cowboy work— roping and riding—and cowboys love it.

There is an art to branding—and cowboys take pride in their art. Everything is done as smooth as silk. The last thing you want is galloping horses and running calves in the branding corral. The cowboys seem so relaxed that it's hard to believe that they're working. But don't let their nonchalance fool you. A top branding team can rope, vaccinate, brand, castrate, and ear mark a calf in less than sixty seconds.

But first, cowboys drive the herds into the corrals, cut out the bulls and put them in separate pens. Then the branding ritual begins. A fire is started and the ranch's branding irons are put in

★ There's an art to branding; the iron can't be too hot or too cold. (*Stephen Collector*) ★

the flames. In the old days, irons were heated over wood fires, but today they're often baked in propane-fueled fires. While the irons are cooking, the knives are sharpened for the ear marking and castration ritual, the syringes are readied for inoculating the calves against bovine sicknesses, and the rust is filed off the dehorning tool.

There's a pecking order at the branding corral. The top hands do the roping. Two ropers compete in the same corral alternating loops; if the first roper's toss misses, the other gets a turn. The peanut gallery watches from the top rail. The old-timers and ranchers wield the cherry-hot irons. Cowboys have to have a sixth sense to tell when a branding iron is not too hot and not too cold, but just right. A hot iron will roast the flesh and could leave a wound, a cold iron will leave a sore spot but no brand. The

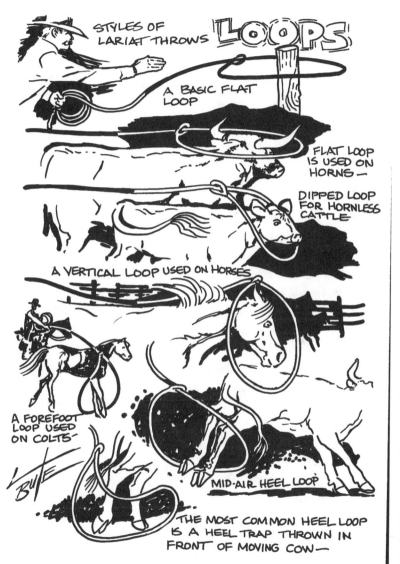

STYLES OF LARIAT THROWS **LOOPS**

A BASIC FLAT LOOP

FLAT LOOP IS USED ON HORNS —

DIPPED LOOP FOR HORNLESS CATTLE

A VERTICAL LOOP USED ON HORSES

A FOREFOOT LOOP USED ON COLTS-

MID-AIR HEEL LOOP

THE MOST COMMON HEEL LOOP IS A HEEL TRAP THROWN IN FRONT OF MOVING COW —

greenhorns, often high school kids, are assigned to the throwing crew, responsible for flopping the calves down once they've been dragged to the fire. If they do it right, they let gravity do the work. If they do it wrong, they go pound for pound with the calf. Often the calf wins. If beginners are smart, they'll keep their eyes open and their mouth shut. One young hand made the mistake of asking which side the brand went on. "We generally like to brand on the outside," the rancher replied.

Cowboy Wisdom

There's more to branding than just getting the job done.

When it's time to start, the ropers swing into the saddle, undo their ropes, and snake out a loop. Alternating tosses, the ropers ease their horses into the herd, single out a calf, heel the hind legs with a loop, dally their rope around the saddle horn, and drag the calf, bawling and kicking, to the ground crew.

At the fire, the flankers, who work in pairs, take over. One takes the rope, the other the tail, as they throw the calf to the ground. Instead of trying to muscle a calf down, veteran flankers use a rhythm that relies on momentum. One places his knee on the calf's neck, the other releases the rope, takes hold of one hind leg and stretches it straight out to keep him from kicking. First comes the vacci-

nation, then the ear mark. The knife man slits the calf's ear and dewlap with a sharp pocketknife. The oval of a calf's ears can be cut into an endless set of designs, which can be seen at a greater distance than a brand. Together, the ear mark and the brand serve as the calf's ID.

In a flash, the brander applies the glowing-hot iron and the hair sizzles. Another takes the dehorning tool and in a round motion digs the two horny nubs out of the calf's skull. Horns can cause injury later on so they're taken off early. Back to the knife man who slices off the tip of the calf's scrotum, pulls out the testicles, and cuts them off. The entire process is over in about a minute, and the calf is turned loose to mother up.

At *vaquero* and buckaroo roundups, the only bipeds are the guys juggling the irons and the knife. Everyone else works on horseback. Ropers work in teams; the first ropes the calf's head; the other hind legs. The head roper eases into the herd, catches a calf around the neck, takes his dallies, and drags it to a spot by the fire. His partner rides up, snaps a loop around the pirouetting calf's hind legs, takes up the slack, dallies, and backs up. In a flick of the wrist, the patient is stretched out, ready for his hot tattoo.

On some ranches they use loading chutes and a branding table where they run the calf through the chute, catch him, and flip him out on a table. When he's done the table flips upright and the calf is released. Some cowmen say that it's easier, but there isn't a cowboy who wouldn't prefer to cut and rope the calves on horseback.

By the time the sun is high overhead, the branding is finished. The cows and calves are left to mother up as the hungry cowboys go wash up. The ranch family will put on a feast for the branding crew and neighbors who stopped by to help. If it's a small place, lunch will be served out of cans from the tailgate of a pickup. If it's a big spread, extra leaves will be put in the dining room table and the platters will be piled high with meat and potatoes and homemade breads.

THE BRANDING RITUAL

BRANDING IRON

RUNNING IRON

CINCH RING

ELECTRIC

FREEZE

DEHORN

BRANDING CHUTE

CALF TABLE

LICE DOSED

VACCINATED

EAR MARKED

CASTRATED

BUTANE BRAND HEATER

DEWCLAWS

BUTE

TRADITIONAL

ROCKY MOUNTAIN OYSTER COLLECTORS

TYPICAL BRANDS

Later, the younger cowboys will go back to the corral to practice team roping and perhaps show off a new horse. After all, rodeo season is just around the corner.

ROCKY MOUNTAIN OYSTERS

Many cow towns and ranches celebrate the rites of spring with a Rocky Mountain Oyster Fry. Where do prairie oysters come from? The branding corral. "Oyster" is actually a euphemism for a calf testicle. You see, just before they're branded, male calves are dehorned and castrated, turned into "steers" rather than bulls. A macho meal at roundup time is a "calf fry" when everyone eats fried calf testicles, washed down with draft beer.

The harvesting of these prairie oysters is dustier than that of the ocean kind. Once the calf has been roped and brought to the branding fire, a cowboy slices off the tip of the scrotum (which is saved to quickly count how many steers were branded), pulls out both testicles, and cuts them off. The testicles are kept in a bucket, to be cleaned and served later in a delicacy known as calf fries or Rocky Mountain oysters.

Back at the ranch, the oysters are washed in cold water and then soaked in buttermilk, coated with batter, and deep fried. That's the basic recipe. But each fanatic has his own carefully guarded recipe that's hauled out once a year. Some cowboys claim that they love the taste of calf fries. Others just gulp and grin. It's sort of a cowboy fertility rite.

Cowboy Wisdom

The man who always
straddles the fence
usually has a sore
crotch.

★

When you get to the
end of your rope, tie a
knot and hang on.

★

★ Roping calves for branding requires a good eye and a deft touch. (*James Fain*) ★

THE FAMILY BRAND

PICKING OUT A brand is serious business, no less so than naming a child. It's cattle country's equivalent of the family's coat of arms. Many cowmen named their ranches after their brand. On my home range, the old Connor place is known as the Lazy S J Ranch. The Smith spread is called the Flying Circle Ranch. The Temples own the Box Lazy L Ranch.

A brand gives a cowman a chance to reflect his feelings, as in FOOL or 2HOT. Some brands travel with the land and cattle. If the ranch is sold, the new owner takes over the brand.

On big ranches, brands are passed down from father to sons. The various sons will distinguish their herds by putting the father's brand on different places on the cows and horses. One might put his brand on the right shoulder. Another will use the left shoulder, the third will use the left hip, and the fourth the right hip. The fifth son or the black sheep of the family sometimes show their independence by picking out their own cattle brand.

Cowmen make their mark with a stamp iron or a running iron. A stamp iron is a pole with the brand on one end and a loop or ring on the other end for hanging on the barn wall. Some nouveau ranchers commission blacksmiths to make them fancy irons, but a true cattleman's iron doesn't look like a rococo fireplace poker. A running iron

★   Cowboys like brands big enough to be read in the moonlight. (*Robin Barker*)   ★

COWBOY CALLIGRAPHY

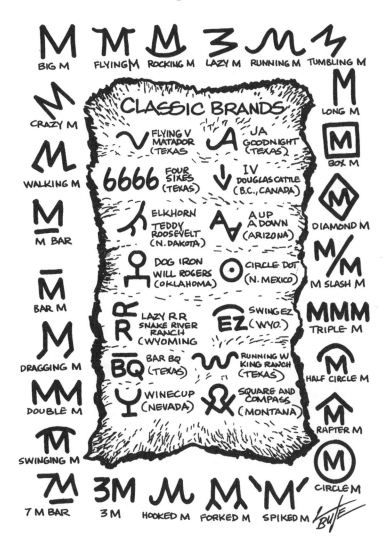

BIG M · **FLYING M** · **ROCKING M** · **LAZY M** · **RUNNING M** · **TUMBLING M**

CRAZY M

WALKING M

M BAR

BAR M

DRAGGING M

DOUBLE M

SWINGING M

7 M BAR · **3 M** · **HOOKED M** · **FORKED M** · **SPIKED M**

LONG M

BOX M

DIAMOND M

M SLASH M

TRIPLE M

HALF CIRCLE M

RAFTER M

CIRCLE M

CLASSIC BRANDS

FLYING V
MATADOR
(TEXAS)

JA
GOODNIGHT
(TEXAS)

6666 FOUR
SIXES
(TEXAS)

IV
DOUGLAS CATTLE
(B.C., CANADA)

ELKHORN
TEDDY
ROOSEVELT
(N. DAKOTA)

A UP
A DOWN
(ARIZONA)

DOG IRON
WILL ROGERS
(OKLAHOMA)

CIRCLE DOT
(N. MEXICO)

LAZY R R
SNAKE RIVER
RANCH
(WYOMING)

SWING EZ
(WYO.)

BAR BQ
(TEXAS)

RUNNING W
KING RANCH
(TEXAS)

WINECUP
(NEVADA)

SQUARE AND
COMPASS
(MONTANA)

BUTE

171

is a big hot pencil for the brand artists to draw his design free-handed.

Besides being seared into the hides of horses and cattle, the family's brand is painted on the front of the barn, printed on the side of the truck, carved into the saddles, traced into wet cement on the new sidewalk, appliqued onto the towels, cut into the crusts of pies ready for the oven. When cowboys talk on the phone, they doodle a brand. Instead of carving their initials into a tree or school desk, country kids scratch their brand.

After something is branded, there's no question to whom it belongs. The first cattleman in North America, Hernando Cortés, burned the letter *G* into his Indian's cheeks and three crosses into the hides of his cattle. "A brand is something that can't come off in the wash" is how my grandfather used to describe it.

Ranchers like big, clear brands, symbols that can be read in the moonlight. They avoid letters and numbers that can be altered by cattle thieves, although rustling is not the problem it once was. With the tip of a running iron a *3* could be turned into a *B* or an *8*. A *C* could be turned into an *O*. And they prefer curves to sharp angles, which tend to blotch and blur the brand.

Cowboys are expected to know and be able to

Cowboy Wisdom

If you work for the man, ride for his brand.

decipher brands (and tell if they've been tampered with). Cowboy calligraphy dicates that brands are read from left to right, from top to bottom, from outside to inside. An "M" in a box is a Box M, not an M Box. And an "M" with a line on top is Bar M.

Besides letters and numbers, every conceivable symbol has been used in a brand: triangles, bells, spurs, bits, hearts, mittens, boots, legs, stars, parachutes, tepees, chairs, even wineglasses. Usually, the shorter the brand, the older the brand. Now when a cowboy decides to get himself a brand, he'll discover that his first choice is already registered. He'll have to use three symbols to make his brand unique in his state.

Brands are registered with the state brand office, which will check its files to see if the brand is available in your county. Several people can have the same brand as long as it's in different locations on the animal and as long as they live in different areas. Inspectors don't want two ranchers with similar brands riding the same range. Horses are only branded once, but cows are branded as often as they're sold. The seller vents or cancels his brand by running a line through it. Then the new owner adds his mark. A cow that's had several owners often looks like a walking billboard.

FOUR-WHEEL FEVER

REAL COWBOYS DRIVE pickup trucks. Not jeeps, not cars—trucks. American-made trucks. It has more to do with practicality than patriotism. Ever try to fit into a Subaru wearing a cowboy hat? A Toyota truck might be fun to drive to the beach but it can't haul a trailer full of horses to the mountains.

A country guy just feels good driving a truck. Cowboy pickups are always four-wheel drives with stick shifts (automatics

are for dudes). That's because they do most of their driving off the pavement. It's not uncommon for cowboys to round up cattle or horses in a beat-up pickup. When a calf makes a beeline away from the herd, the cowboy will gun the motor, stomp on the gas pedal, and give chase. Sometimes the critter wins, as when a calf jumps down a steep bluff. The cowboy slams on his brakes, cusses, and mutters that maybe the cattle

★ Cowboy Cadillac. (*Stephen Collector*) ★

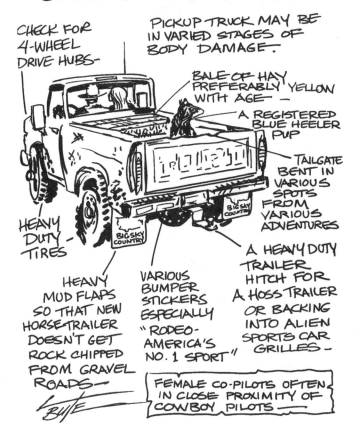

HOW TO IDENTIFY COWBOY SPACECRAFT

CHECK FOR 4-WHEEL DRIVE HUBS-

PICKUP TRUCK MAY BE IN VARIED STAGES OF BODY DAMAGE.

BALE OF HAY PREFERABLY YELLOW WITH AGE -

A REGISTERED BLUE HEELER PUP

TAILGATE BENT IN VARIOUS SPOTS FROM VARIOUS ADVENTURES

HEAVY DUTY TIRES

BIG SKY COUNTRY

A HEAVY DUTY TRAILER HITCH FOR A HOSS TRAILER OR BACKING INTO ALIEN SPORTS CAR GRILLES -

HEAVY MUD FLAPS SO THAT NEW HORSE-TRAILER DOESN'T GET ROCK CHIPPED FROM GRAVEL ROADS-

VARIOUS BUMPER STICKERS ESPECIALLY "RODEO-AMERICA'S NO. 1 SPORT"

FEMALE CO-PILOTS OFTEN IN CLOSE PROXIMITY OF COWBOY PILOTS -

are getting smarter. Then again, maybe it's his rig.

According to Michael Martin Murphey's song, you've got "Cowboy Logic" if you can figure out which of the three guys in hats and boots sitting together in the front seat of the pickup is the genuine item. (Answer: The real cowboy's the one in the middle; the guy on the left is stuck driving and the guy on the right has to hop out and open the gate.)

Four-wheel-drive pickups with all the options are affectionately called "cowboy Cadillacs." They cost in the neighborhood of $27,000. But a cowboy gets his money out of a truck. He'll drive it into the ground and replace the engine once or twice before he declares it dead.

Playing cowboys and engines is a favorite pastime. Truck brands have long since replaced the Protestant denominations as the major religions on the range. Men who drive Ford Lariat XLTs, for example, are aligned by the same set of wheels. Conservative ranchers tend to drive Fords or Chevys.

RULES OF THE DIRT ROAD

• A cowboy waves when another vehicle passes by, whether he recognizes it or not. The wave may be little more than raising two fingers in the air.

• A cowboy keeps the windows rolled down and the air conditioner off.

• A cowboy rolls up the windows when he sees a cloud of dust coming at him.

• A cowboy wears his seat belt only when his wife or kid reminds him to.

• A cowboy drives a

COWBOY ROAD LANGUAGE—

COWBOYS WAVE AT MOST DRIVERS ON COUNTRY ROADS OUT OF HABIT—

← A CASUAL WAVE IS COMMON COURTESY IN THE RURAL WEST—

ONE DIGIT— "KNOWN YOU ALL OF MY LIFE."

TWO DIGIT— "I'LL PAY MY FEED BILL NEXT WEEK."

THREE DIGIT— "I KNOW YOU'RE NOT LOCAL."

THREE MISSING DIGITS— "HI, I'M A DALLY ROPER."

stick shift, not an automatic.

- A cowboy stops in the middle of the road to chew the fat with friends and neighbors coming the opposite direction.

- A cowboy never drives the speed limit when he's close to home. He slows down to check out the neighbor's operation—the condition of his fields, his fences, his equipment, and his livestock.

- A cowboy brakes for livestock. If he recognizes the brand, he'll chase them back into the field where they belong. If they're far from home, he'll call their owner to come and get 'em.

Flashy rodeo riders are more apt to drive up in a Dodge truck with custom stripes. (Dodge is one of the big rodeo sponsors.)

A respected judge in the prosperous ranching town of Dillon, Montana, once defined cowboy ambition: "He wants a truck with a dog and a bale of hay in the back, a ten-gallon hat, and a wife who works in the courthouse."

RANCH CUISINE

COWBOYS ARE CAR-NIVORES. They'll eat chicken when they're sick, pork for variety, fish if they caught it, but a day without beef is a day without sunshine. But no old-time cowman liked the taste of his own beef. In fact, he took pride in never eating a cow with his own brand on it. Cowboys like to tell the old story about a rancher who got his neighbor to invite him to dinner so he could see what his own beef tasted like.

Times have changed. Now when a ranch family needs beef, they round up a couple of steers, bring them in, and fatten them. Then they put them in a horse trailer and drop them off at the local slaughterhouse. The butcher calls the family cook and discusses how she wants the beef cut: how thick the steaks, how big the roasts, how many pounds in each package of hamburger. When the meat's ready, they haul it home for the family freezer, which is often the size of a horse trailer.

Cowboys like chicken-fried steaks (look what frying can do for the lowly chicken) or grilled steaks, cooked clean through. Whenever my father is served a steak that's too rare, he'll say, "Quick, call the vet, maybe he can save it." He's not joking. There's one old story about a cowboy who ordered a steak in a Kansas City restaurant. When the steak arrived at the table pink, he sent it back to the kitchen with "I've seen cows get well that was hurt worse than that."

Cowboy Wisdom

Nothing helps scenery like steak and eggs.

Chili's a lot like sex: When it's good, it's great, and when it's bad, it's not so bad.

steaks are pierced on the end of each fork tine and then lowered into the hot suet. If he's cooking for a big branding party, rancher Steve Jackson will cook four steaks on each tine, or sixteen at a time.

Anyone who's ever braved the meat counter walks away wondering what makes a good steak. Here's the answer straight from the cowboy's mouth: a two-year-old, 1,200-pound steer fed on good grain and hay. They may be born in Wyoming or Texas, but the best cattle in the world reach maturity at feed lots in Iowa, Nebraska, or outside Chicago. Then the top-choice steaks are sent back to steak houses in Fort Worth or Kaycee.

Even though there are only about ninety pounds of steak in a thousand-pound steer, steaks are the most popular cuts of beef. Steak comes from an old Saxon word, "steak," meaning "meat on a stick." We think of barbecue as a Texas invention but actually the Saxons were the first to cook steak on a stick over a campfire. Cowboys are fond of pitchfork steaks. Pitchfork steak parties are cattle country's version of a fondue party. But instead of sticks, the cook uses a pitchfork. The oil is heated in an enormous cast iron kettle suspended from a chain over a log fire. Sirloin

What should you look for when you're picking out a steak? Cowboys look for marbling, the flecks of fat within the lean. The top-graded steaks, called "Prime" by the USDA, have the most marbling. Marbling makes beef tender and gives that extra burst of flavor when you take a bite. City folks worried about their arteries often choose leaner meat, but in a cowboy's mind, they're missing the boat. Lean meat can taste like boot leather.

Meat without marbling is like coffee without the caffeine. It looks like beef, smells like beef, but it doesn't taste the way beef should taste.

Ask a cowboy his favorite steak and nine times out of ten he'll vote for sirloin. Actually a cut of tenderloin, the steak was named by a British monarch. His highness was so overwhelmed by a good loin steak that he put down his napkin, pulled out his sword, and dubbed it "Sir Loin."

When there's lots of work to be done and the cowboys might not be back before dusk, the ranch cook will serve steak and eggs for breakfast. A sturdy cowboy can fill up at breakfast and go all day until supper if he has to. If he's trying to stave off hunger pains, he'll dig deep into his saddlebag for cowboy fast food—beef jerky, dried fruit, nuts—which can be eaten with one hand. He needs the other hand to hold the reins.

At the end of the day, horses pick up the pace as they sense the nearness of the barn and the cool meadow beyond. And cowboys tune up their taste buds, knowing that dinner is ready and waiting.

★ Cookie can prepare a feast on an open fire. (*Bar T Five*) ★

Here are a couple of recipes that will make a cowboy fall in love.

RANCH-STYLE CHICKEN-FRIED STEAK

When ranch cooks fry steaks, they cook enough to feed a branding crew. I've cut this recipe down to family size.

2 lbs. round steak, cut into 4 pieces
½ cup flour
1½ tsps. salt
½ tsp. pepper
½ cup milk
½ cup oil
2 cups milk (if no one's counting calories, some cooks use part whipping cream)

Trim fat from steaks and save. Mix together flour, salt, and pepper in a small bowl. Sprinkle over meat. Pound each side with a meat hammer until it offers no more resistance. Dip in milk and then flour mixture. Heat oil and trimmed fat in deep frying pan over high heat. Fry steaks about five minutes each side until golden brown. Remove steak from pan and place in a warm oven while you finish the gravy. Pour off fat, leaving about ¼ cup in pan. Add ¼ cup flour and cook over low heat until a paste forms. Add milk. Stir and cook until thickened for gravy. Don't mind the lumps. Serve over steak. Makes 4 servings.

ROUNDUP POT ROAST WITH BLACK GRAVY

5 lb. pot roast, at least 2 inches thick
2 tsps. salt
2 Tbs. shortening
1 kettle of boiling water
½ cup coffee
3–4 Tbs. cornstarch

Rub meat with salt. Melt shortening in a heavy Dutch oven. Brown roast in hot fat over medium heat, turning once. When browned on both sides, add 1 cup of boiling water. Cover and cook over low heat for about 3 hours, either on the stove or in the oven at 325°F. Add hot water each time the pot is almost dry. When the roast is almost done, add hot coffee instead of water. When the meat is well done (use a meat thermometer or fork to test), remove from the Dutch oven and keep hot. Add 2 to 3 cups hot water and scrape all the tar off the bottom of the pan. Thicken with cornstarch. Season with salt and pepper to taste. Bring to a boil, reduce heat, and simmer for 5 minutes. Serve with mashed potatoes, fresh vegetables, biscuits, fruit salad, and two kinds of pie.

THE BEST STEAK HOUSES"

Only a rank degenerate would drive 1,500 miles across Texas without eating a chicken-fried steak," writes Larry McMurtry in *In a Narrow Grave: Essays on Texas.* "It would be like going to Italy and not trying the pasta." And no one travels in cattle country like rodeo cowboys, who can easily put 100,000 miles on their trucks in one season. When cowboys sit down to eat, they have their minds on one thing: steak. "Whoever wins the most money in Houston has to buy the steaks in San Angelo," says Ote Berry, a world champion steer wrestler. When cowboys order beef, they ask for prime rib as thick as a family roast, sirloin steaks the size of Rhode Island, and chicken-fried steaks smothered in gravy. Of course, they order their steaks well done (as opposed to still mooing).

A herd of rodeo riders at the National Finals Rodeo was asked to reveal their favorite steak houses on the suicide circuit. Here are their top choices:

The Big Texan
P.O. Box 37000, Amarillo, TX
(806-372-7000)

Hungry as a bear? The Big Texan serves steaks the size of Texas. Beef is on the house if you can eat a 72 oz. steak in an hour. Sounds impossible, but one out of eight customers gets a freebie. Besides steaks, the restaurant offers entertainment—melodramas, opry, rodeos, and a cowboy morning breakfast complete with cowboy poetry.

Binion's Ranch Steak House
128 Fremont, Las Vegas, NV
(702-382-1600)

Founder Benny Binion, one of rodeo's biggest supporters, created a cowboy oasis inside his Horseshoe Casino. The wood-paneled restaurant serves stiff drinks, prime beef, and great desserts. One of the specialties is Benny's Cut, a 20 oz. slab of prime rib.

Del Frisco's Double Eagle Steak House
4300 Lemmon Ave., Dallas, TX
(214-526-9811)

With a wine list as long as a rodeo roster, Del Frisco's is a cut above your average steak house. Steak lover's heaven, it offers everything from filet mignon to porterhouse steaks, as well as carpetbag steak, governor's filet, and Santa Fe Peppercorn steak.

The Golden Ox
1600 Genessee Street,
Kansas City, MO
(816-842-2866)

Located in the livestock exchange building behind the old stockyards, the Golden Ox used to cater to cowboys celebrating the end of a trail drive. Today rodeo riders say that this is the real reason why Kansas City is still famous for its steaks.

The Hole in the Wall
Kaycee, WY (307-738-2374)

Named after Butch Cassidy's gang, this hole in the wall is a favorite of Wyoming cowboys. Try its rib-eye steaks or top sirloin.

Land of Magic
11060 Front St., Logan, near
Manhattan, MT (406-284-3794)

Charbroiled steaks are served at this log restaurant in the heart of cow country. Every year the owner sponsors a branding party where local ranchers stop by with their irons and leave their mark on the wall. Most stay to eat.

Cowboy Wisdom

Pasta isn't a main dish at

any meal.

Smuggler's Inn
6920 MacLeod Trail S.,
Calgary, Alberta (403-253-5355)

Here's where Alberta cowboys eat Alberta beef, fresh not frozen. Its specialties are sirloin steaks and prime rib for diners with horse-size appetites. Smuggler's does no advertising. It doesn't have to. Word of mouth travels fast. The place is packed during the Calgary Stampede and the annual bull sale in February.

Western Skies
2020 N. Chadborn, San Angelo, TX
(915-655-3610)

Winners at the Houston rodeo pick up the checks when riders feast at Western Skies. It's famous for its Kansas City strip steak, served family style.

CHAPTER TWENTY-ONE

LET'S RODEO

THERE'S NO DENY-ING that rodeo weekend is *the* social event of the year in Western towns. And the smaller the town, the less pretentious and more genuine the rodeo. It has all the energy of a street fair, all the hoopla of the circus coming to town.

The fighting spirit that tamed the West still survives in the rodeo arena. Old-time bronc busters had to master green horses on the open plains. Roundups

★ You can't beat rodeo for high drama. Here a cowboy checks out from a horse called Heidelberg. *(James Fain)* ★

were a chance for ropers to show off their horses and their dallies. Today, ranchers, cowboys, and weekend rangers look forward to rodeo week all year long. There's always a good parade: a horse-drawn wagon, a local saddle club, cowboys in leather, cowgirls in sequins, a high school marching band tiptoeing through the horse apples left behind. Seated on the back of an old convertible, the local politician waves back and forth like a windshield wiper.

People come out in droves to watch the riding and roping feats. The grandstands are filled with friends and neighbors, while the bars are filled with buddies and babes. There's bound to be a fistfight or two. And at the Saturday night dance, it's a sure bet that the band will play "My Heroes Have Always Been Cowboys." (Maybe two or three times.)

The festive atmosphere of the town provides the backdrop for the thrills of rodeo. Unlike other sports, there's always an element of danger, the opportunity for high drama: A cowboy can get gored by a vengeful bull or hung up on a bucking bronc. Last summer a Brahman bull broke out of the rodeo arena in Billings, Montana, crashed though the parking lot, and hid out in a city park. For five weeks the city was on a full bull alert. When the bull was finally captured, he was renamed "Longtimenosee."

Along with the thrills, freedom and friendship are still what draws young cowboys to the rodeo

Cowboy Wisdom

Top riders never say "can't" or "don't."

Riding a bronc is like dancing with a girl. The trick is matching your partner's rhythm.

★

life. "My grandpa used to tell me to save every buckle and meet every one you can," recalls bronc rider Derek Clark. "Because when you're done, that's all you're going to have left." The rodeo arena has been the place where many young cowboys have come of age, proving themselves in front of the whole town. If the kid rides to the whistle, he'll earn the whole town's applause. If he's dumped in the dust and walks away, he will still earn their applause.

Rodeo contests fall into two categories: rough stock events, which depend on balance and endurance, and timed events, which depend on skill and speed. Rough stock events include Saddle Bronc Riding, rodeo's classic contest, Bareback Bronc Riding, the fan's favorite competition, and Bull Riding, the most dangerous event. Timed events include Calf Roping, Steer Wrestling, Team Roping, and Ladies Barrel Racing. Each rodeo committee may add some other events, depending on the age of the cowboys and the region.

Saddle bronc riding demands superb balance and flamboyant style, more than brute strength.

The rider has to find the bucking bronc's rhythm and swing with it for the whole ride. He can't touch the animal with his free hand or he's disqualified. He can't wave his hat the way Gene Autry used to. He has to spur every time the horse jumps. And he has to stay on until the eight-second whistle blows.

Bareback riders, who are denied reins or a saddle, are judged on their spurring technique and control. They're anchored to the horse with little more than a suitcase handle. A top rider can spur the fur off a grizzly bear. But when you're flopping and popping, it's harder to spur. "It's hard to sit up and be in control," says Larry Sandvick. "I like to stay back and let 'er roll."

In bull riding, niceties like technique are thrown out the barn window. The point is merely to survive. Bulls are

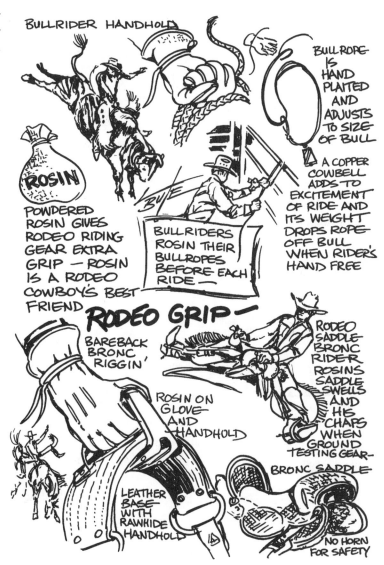

BULLRIDER HANDHOLD

BULL ROPE IS HAND PLAITED AND ADJUSTS TO SIZE OF BULL

A COPPER COWBELL ADDS TO EXCITEMENT OF RIDE AND ITS WEIGHT DROPS ROPE OFF BULL WHEN RIDER'S HAND FREE

ROSIN

POWDERED ROSIN GIVES RODEO RIDING GEAR EXTRA GRIP — ROSIN IS A RODEO COWBOY'S BEST FRIEND

BULLRIDERS ROSIN THEIR BULLROPES BEFORE EACH RIDE —

RODEO GRIP —

BAREBACK BRONC RIGGIN'

ROSIN ON GLOVE AND HANDHOLD

RODEO SADDLE BRONC RIDER ROSINS SADDLE SWELLS AND HIS CHAPS WHEN GROUND TESTING GEAR

BRONC SADDLE

LEATHER BASE WITH RAWHIDE HANDHOLD

NO HORN FOR SAFETY

bigger and stronger than broncs and they have more moves. Cowboys have to anticipate spins, jumps, twists, drops, and tilts, all done at machine-gun speed. Bull riders are the slickest dressers, the biggest spenders, the heaviest gamblers, the hardest drinkers—the macho men of rodeo. Ambitious cowgirls always prefer a bull rider, a twister, for a boyfriend.

Anyone with guts and luck can ride a bucking bronc or bull, but it takes years of practice to be proficient with a rope. That's one reason why bronc and bull riders tend to be younger and greener, while ropers tend to be older and grayer. The best bronc riders tend to come from up north, while the best ropers and wrestlers come from the Southwest. With dozens of champs to its credit, little Checotah, Oklahoma, calls itself the steer wrestling capital of the world.

The top cowboys belong to the Professional Rodeo Cowboys Association. The PRCA writes the rules, sanctions the rodeos, recruits sponsors, and promotes rodeo. All this bureaucracy is fairly new to cowboys. They didn't even have a union un-

Cowboy Wisdom

The family that rodeos together plays together —and prays together.

★

A bucket of luck when you need it is better than a truckload of talent.

★

til 1936, when cowboys competing at a rodeo at the Boston Garden went on strike until they were ensured more prize money and fair judging. The group called itself the "Cowboys' Turtle Association," because of members' slow-moving efforts to band together. Its successor, the PRCA, sanctions about eight hundred rodeos a year and oversees twelve rodeo circuits, where regional cowboys can compete close to home.

But for cowboys intent on winning the world championship, the commute isn't easy: in one rodeo, out the gate, and down the road to the next night's competition, a state or two away. They see more of the road than rodeos. Surviving on coffee and catnaps, they get used to the hum of the horse trailer on all-night drives, endless miles of highway, and slept-in clothes. By summer's end they have seen every road sign a couple of times, and know the truck stops like they know the bucking chutes. Most cowboys find it impossible to hit all the rodeos they'd like to. To make it easier on the wallet and the driver, the PRCA allows cowboys to enter as a

★   A bull rider survives his partner from hell as the bullfighter comes running to the rescue.
(*Mark MacLeod*) ★

group for the same performance so that they can share traveling expenses.

"Most cowboys hardly make more money than they spend," says Cody Lambert, a bull rider and saddle bronc rider. Rodeo riders pay their own entry fees and travel costs, which easily eat up half of the their winnings. The good cowboys earn their fees back plus a little pocket money; the majority break even after expenses. The all-around champ is the cowboy who's won the most money. In order to fill his saddlebags with cash, he has to compete in two or three events.

It's a cowboy crap shoot. The luck of the draw is essential. There's little a cowboy can do to dress up a horse or bull that performs badly or to prevent a calf or steer from running along the fence or a steer from dropping his horns. Each time a rough stock rider blasts out of the chute, he risks getting hurt and going broke all at once. If he does go broke, there's no one else to blame. That's probably why rodeo cowboys are loners, proud of being able to do everything by themselves. "Rodeo is a sport where you can be your own boss, go to as many or as few rodeos as you want, when you want," says bareback champ Clint Corey.

Considering the odds, it's fitting that the National Finals Rodeo is held every December in Las Vegas. "It doesn't get any better than this,"

Cowboy Wisdom

How do you get to Las Vegas? Practice, practice, practice.

says bull rider Jim Sharp. "The greatest cowboys in the world get bucked off the greatest bulls and broncs." Las Vegas is like a Super Bowl, family reunion, trade convention, and great party rolled into one. But the NFR riders don't party. For them, Las Vegas could mean the difference between hitting the jackpot or just barely breaking even. Many winners make more money in the ten days in December than they have made all season.

Ask ten rodeo riders what they plan to do after they retire from rodeo, and all ten will tell you that they hope to ranch. "I've been buying land and cows and horses," says Cody Lambert. "I'm trying to put a little ranch together. Hopefully I'll make enough in rodeo to be able to be a rancher, still be my own boss, and make my own decisions."

THE SUICIDE CIRCUIT

For eleven months a year, rodeo cowboys "go down the road," travelling from major league rodeos in Calgary or Cheyenne to dusty corrals in Helmville, Montana, or Tucumcari, New Mexico. The pace is as grueling as the actual sport. Entering more than 125 rodeos a year is not uncommon. That means one a week during the winter and one every day in the summer.

Here are the top fifteen rodeos, the biggest contests with the biggest purses:

January	National Western Stock Show and Rodeo	Denver, CO
January	Southwestern Exposition & Livestock Show & Rodeo	Fort Worth, TX
February	San Antonio Livestock Exposition Rodeo	San Antonio, TX
Feburary	Houston Livestock Show & Rodeo	Houston, TX
February	La Fiesta de Los Vaqueros	Tucson, AZ
March	Dodge National Circuit Finals Rodeo	Pocatello, ID
June	Reno Rodeo	Reno, NV
July	Calgary Stampede	Calgary, AB
July	California Rodeo	Salinas, CA
July	Cheyenne Frontier Days Rodeo	Cheyenne, WY
September	New Mexico State Fair Rodeo	Albuquerque, NM
September	Pendleton Roundup Rodeo	Pendleton, OR
October	Grand National Rodeo	San Francisco, CA
December	National Finals Rodeo	Las Vegas, NV

RODEO TALK

Besides "yep" and "nope," here's what you'll need to know to appreciate the action in the rodeo arena:

ASSOCIATION SADDLE. The standard hornless bronc saddle.

AVERAGE. The contestant with the highest cumulative score or lowest total time wins the event.

BAREBACK RIGGING. The suitcase handle that anchors the bareback rider to his bronc.

BICYCLING. Spurring with one foot and then the other, like riding a bicycle.

BLOWING A STIRRUP. When a bronc rider loses a stirrup, which means that he's disqualified.

BREAKING THE BARRIER. In timed events, steers and calves are given a head start. If a contestant rides through the rope barrier before it's released, he's given a ten-second penalty.

BUCKLE BUNNIES. Rodeo groupies.

BULL FIGHTER. Once known as the rodeo clown.

BULL ROPE. A flat braided rope that circles the bull's chest. The bull

★ Bull fighters, the only cowboys who don't wear boots, are the gymnasts of the rodeo world.
(*Stephen Collector*) ★

rider slips his glove under the rope and hangs on.

COASTING. Riding all the way with your feet on the horse's shoulders, instead of spurring.

DAYLIGHTING. If a calf is lying down when the roper arrives, he must lift the calf off the ground before it can be tied.

DINK. A bucking horse with a poor reputation. Since the animal's performance counts for half the cowboy's score, he doesn't want to draw a dink.

DOGGER. A steer wrestler.

DRAW. The judges have a drawing and match riders with rough stock. Rodeo cowboys always talk about the luck of the draw.

DUSTED. Bucked off by a bronc or bull.

FISHING. When a roper accidentally makes a legal catch.

FLANK STRAP. A sheepskinlined strap that goes around the flank of a bucking horse or bull. It causes no pain, but encourages the animal to buck.

GO-ROUND. One round of a multiday contest.

GOLD BUCKLE. Rodeo's gold medal.

★ A bareback rider takes his licks.
(*James Fain*) ★

HAZER. A steer wrestler's mounted assistant. His job is to keep the steer running in a straight line until the contestant leaves his horse and takes hold of its horns.

HEART. The desire to win. A top rider has to have heart.

HOOKER. A bull that uses its horns to try to dump a rider.

HUNG UP. When a cowboy's foot is caught in a stirrup or his hand is entangled in the bareback rigging or bull rope.

MARK. Position of a rider's feet. When the bronc comes out of the chute, the rider's feet must be placed above the point of the horse's shoulder.

PIGGIN' STRING. A short, slender rope that calf ropers use to tie a calf's feet. They hold it between their teeth as they ride out of the chute.

PULLING LEATHER. If a bronc rider grabs the saddle, he's automatically disqualified.

RAKING. The art of spurring a bronc. The rider swings his legs back and forth, from the horse's shoulders to its rump.

RANK HORSE. A bronc that's tough, unpredictable, and knows how to buck.

RERIDE. A cowboy gets a second chance on another animal if the judges decide he wasn't given a fair shot (maybe his horse didn't buck or it stumbled or fell).

SCRATCHING. Another word for raking.

SEEING DAYLIGHT. When a saddle bronc rider is bucked out of the saddle.

SPINNER. A bull that spins like a whirling dervish.

TAKING HIS LICKS. The downward spurring action of a bronc rider each time the horse kicks up its back legs.

TRY. Guts and determination.

WELL. The area inside a spinning bull.

THE BUCKS START HERE

A BRONC RIDER faces the moment of truth when he climbs on the hurricane deck. He will get, in the words of Charles M. Russell, "a fine chance to study hoss enitimy from under and over." No two horses buck the same way—each has his own special combo to send a rider picking daisies. But many bucks are recognizable. Bronc riders spend hours studying how rank horses buck. "It helps to know how the horse comes out of the chute, whether it fires right away or comes out and then bucks," says one bronc rider. Here's a chute boss's guide to bucking broncs:

BLIND BUCKER is a dangerous draw. This horse doesn't give a damn where he bucks and will buck into or through anything.
CROW HOPPER is one of the easiest broncs. He puts on an act by arching his back and jumping up stiff-legged, but his heart's not in it.
HIGH ROLLER is a horse that leaps high into the air when bucking. He always gives a good ride and a good show.
PILE DRIVER is a terrific bucker. The bronc jumps into the air and comes down stiff-legged, giving the rider a jolt hard enough to rattle his teeth, if not his brains.
PUMP HANDLE is a horse that bucks like a seesaw. He gives an easy ride and a low score.
SIDEWINDER is a horse that gives a sharp turn or twist after he has jumped into the air. Most times, the horse goes one way and the cowboy sails the other.
SPINNER bucks as it whirls and twirls. Usually the rider gets dizzy, loses his grip, and sails off.
SUNFISHER is a horse that raises its

front legs off the ground and then leaps forward, landing with one shoulder much lower than the other. When sunlight hits its belly, the cowboy hits the ground.

STRAIGHTAWAY BUCKER looks easy, but don't let him fool you. Big and strong, he bucks straight down the center without any twists. But when he starts to land, he kicks again with his hind legs, throwing his rider high and hard.

Cowboy Wisdom

When you climb into the saddle, you'd better be prepared to ride.

If the rodeo doesn't kill you , the commute will.

★ Bareback champ Harry Tompkins had the right stuff. So did his bronc. (*PRCA*) ★

ALL BULL, NO B.S.

The bull riders get all the glory but the bulls do half the work. Here's an insider's look at one of the rank bulls:

NAME: OKEECHOBEE FATS

AGE: 6

COLOR: Red-and-white paint

WEIGHT: 2,200 pounds

EXPERIENCE: Bucked professionally for 3 years

TRIPS TO NFR: 2

SCORE: Always in the 90s

OWNER: Beutler and Gaylord Rodeo Co., Elk City, OK

BUILD: Wide body. Bull riders sometimes have a hard time getting their legs down on him. "He must be three feet across his back," says owner Bennie Beutler.

REPUTATION: Known as a bullrider's bull

MEANNESS: "After the ride, he's real gentle," assures Beutler. "He won't go out of his way to hook anybody."

SIXTH SENSE: Can recognize a champion bull rider. "He can feel the confidence of a Tuff Hedeman or a Teddy Nuce," says Beutler. "Has his best trips when the best cowboys are on him because he works harder."

MOTIVATION: Might not buck as hard when a permit holder is on his back. Less of a challenge.

BEST TRIPS: Dumped two cowboys at the 1992 NFR. Gave Charlie Sampson a 90-point winning ride at 1992 Denver rodeo.

RODEO SCHOOLS

★ Bronc riding requires rhythm and stamina. Here a rider masters a pile driver.
(*Mark MacLeod*) ★

Rodeo riders earn their stripes in the arena, but many learn their skills at rodeo school, boot camps for would-be performers. Rodeo schools, put on by ex-champs and current gold buckle winners, are where the best and the toughest hone their technique or get back in the saddle after a bad accident. Some schools even cater to city cowboys who want to learn how to rodeo. Where else would a Tallahassee tenderfoot or a Durham dude learn how to ride a bull?

Rodeo teachers insist that they would rather tutor a greenhorn how to ride than coach a rider who has developed a lot of bad habits. "One year we had eight women at our bronc riding school," says Shawn Davis, former saddle bronc champion and head of the rodeo program at the College of Southern Idaho in Twin Falls. Top teachers like Davis, who has been general manager of the National Finals Rodeo, are so revered by their students that they're the only cowboys called "Mister."

Unless a cowboy grew up riding steers and breaking horses, rodeo school is a prerequisite before riding rough stock. Students attend lectures, watch tapes of NFR events, practice on a bucking machine or mechanical steer before it's their turn to saddle up. "We teach the students safety techniques— how to set your rigging on a horse, how to get on a bucking bronc," explains Davis. The machines simulate the action so we can show people how to safely get on and off a bronc. All the dos and don'ts." Greenhorns practice the fundamentals on gentle stock, what cowboys call "pups" or "the nice ones," before they take on the rank stock. Some rookies catch on really quick, while others never get used to it. It comes down to natural talent and the old cowboy try—teeth-gritting determination. That's why some cowboys insist that nobody can teach you to ride— you're born to ride.

Conquering the fear is the biggest hurdle for most newcomers. It's like learning to swim," says Butch Myers, former steer wrestling champ. "You've just got to dive in." One teacher likens a rider's first trip to the bucking chute to bungee jumping. "At first it's a blur," says Lewis Feild, former all-around cowboy champ. "It's like driving 190 MPH."

You'll need to bring your own equipment— glove, chaps, saddle, rigging, rope. Teachers will make sure that your gear is set right for you. Some schools will rent gear or lend stuff (let them know ahead of time if you need gear). Make sure that your health insurance is up to date. (You ride at your own risk.) And don't forget your hat.

Here's a short list of the best rodeo schools:

RODEO SCHOOL

College of Southern Idaho, Box 1238,
Twin Falls, ID 83301
(208-733-9554)

Shawn Davis, former saddle bronc champion and general manager of the NFR, is the man in charge. He offers two rodeo schools, one in December for beginners and another in March. Davis's stock includes animals for beginners, intermediates, and advanced riders. "We would never put a beginner on a rank animal," he says. "After a few rides, if they relax and ride good, we graduate them up to better stock." CSI is big on the basics. "If you have the fundamentals down pat, you can improve," says Davis.

BUTCH MYERS
Athens, TX
(903-675-1532)

Myers, a former steer wrestling champ, offers one of the best steer wrestling and calf roping schools. Students practice on dummy calves and steers before taking on real live animals.

GARY LEFFEW
Santa Maria, CA
(805-929-4286)

Leffew, the thinking man's cowboy, puts on a popular bull-riding school. Leffew rode his first bull at a rodeo. A year later he was riding full time. A seven-time NFR bull rider, Leffew won the championship in 1970. His theory stresses mental preparation as well as physical fitness. Students are taught to ride bulls in their minds, as well as actual technique.

LEWIS FEILD
Elk Ridge, UT
(901-465-4347)

Rodeo champ turned stock contractor, Feild offers bareback-riding and saddle-bronc-riding schools at his ranch in Utah, using his own rough stock.

TRIPLE CROSS RANCH
Davie, FL
(305-474-1172)

Owners Norman and Phyllis Edwards recruit champs like Walt Woodward (team roping), Cody Custer (bull riding), and Mike Fletcher (bareback riding) to teach rodeo school at their Florida ranch.

GOLD BUCKLE RODEO SCHOOLS
Biddle, MT
(406-427-5290)

Producer Tim Jones puts on rodeo schools, taught by gold buckle champs, in Billings, Montana; Spring Valley, Minnesota; and Miller Grove, Texas.

ROPING AGAINST THE CLOCK

CALF ROPING, LIKE bronc riding, was born on the ranches of the Old West. Calves were roped and then flopped down so they could be branded or doctored. Ranch cowboys still rope calves in their day-to-day work, which is why so many hometown cowboys compete at the local rodeo.

Calf roping is a lot harder than it sounds. First off, the calf gets a head start—up to twenty feet, depending on the size of the arena. To discourage ropers from jumping the gun, a ten second penalty is added if they break the barrier. A cowboy's success depends on the teamwork with his horse and the luck of the draw. A feisty calf that runs fast or kicks hard can foil the best-tossed loop. The rope horse must overtake and match speeds with the calf. Riding at full gallop, the cowboy attempts to rope the calf around the neck and dismount on the run. (Two throws are allowed.) The impact of the horse coming to a sliding stop usually pulls the calf to the ground. While the horse keeps the rope taut, the cowboy runs to the calf, throws it down, and ties three legs of the squirming 250-pound animal with a short piece of rope, called a piggin' string (which he's been holding in his teeth). Time is declared when the cowboy throws up his hands. But the game is not yet over. The calf has to stay tied for six seconds after the roper remounts his horse and loosens the slack on the rope. If the calf wiggles himself loose, the cowboy rides home empty-handed. Winning time: eight to ten seconds.

A rope horse's skills are as important as the roper's. The horse must be fast, smart, and able to stop on a dime. A good rope horse holds, rider or no rider, never allowing the calf to get a side run on him or give the rope an inch of slack. Highly prized, rodeo rope horses are worth

thousands of dollars. The horse's owner often rents it out to several competitors for a share of the prize money.

Dean Oliver of Boise, Idaho, is considered by many to have been the greatest calf roper of all time. He won the world calf roping championship eight times in a row. Two broken catch ropes cost him his ninth title at the 1966 NFR. That taught him to

★ A top calf roper makes the catch look easy. (*Mark MacLeod*) ★

always check his ropes. In calf roping, there is no margin for error.

One of the toughest events, steer wrestling is hard on the back pockets of Wranglers. A cowboy must leap from a speeding quarter horse going thirty-five miles an hour onto the horns of a seven-hundred-pound steer and wrestle it to the ground. Technique is everything is this event.

Invented by a black cowboy named Bill Pickett, steer wrestling used to be called bulldogging. One day Pickett got mad at a steer he was trying to drive into a corral at a Texas ranch and he grabbed the animal's horns, sunk his teeth into his lip like a bulldog, and wrestled it to the ground. Calling himself "The Dusky Demon," Pickett took his act on the road, touring with the Miller 101 Wild West Show. His bite-'em-cowboy trick brought the steers to the

HORNS OF PLENTY

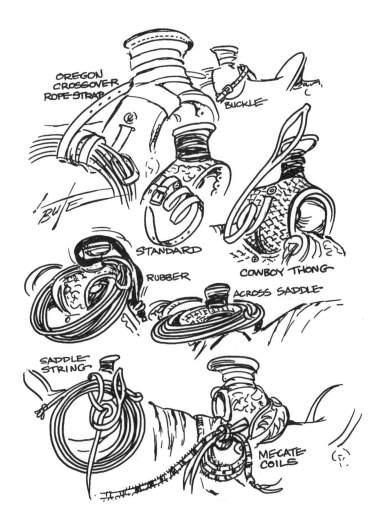

ground and the crowd to their feet—every time.

They may still be called bull-doggers (doggers, for short), but steer wrestlers today wouldn't think of biting a steer. They use the law of gravity to bring the animal to the ground.

As in calf roping, the steer is released with a head start, tripping the barrier for two cowboys—the dogger and the hazer—to pursue. The hazer's job is to crowd the steer and keep him running in a straight line. The steer can run faster than almost anything on four legs, except the quarter horses that most cowboys use. The steer, the dogger, and the hazer break from behind a barrier and run hell-bent down the arena until the dogger is ready to make his play. Holding onto the saddle horn with one hand, he uses the other to grab the steer's horn. When the steer's head is in the crook of his armpit, he lets himself down. The trick is for the dogger to time his leap so that the horse's momentum sweeps his legs out in front of the steer

Cowboy Wisdom

Team roping is like marriage. It requires commitment to make it work.

The horse gets all the glory but the roper gets all the money.

Steer wrestlers aren't hesitant about throwing their weight around.

★

where he can dig in his heels and brake for a stop. If he dives too soon, he'll get dragged along. All he can do is to hold onto the steer's hair and hope for a soft landing.

When the steer stops, the dogger wrestles the animal down. Time is declared when the 600-pound steer is on its side with four feet pointing in the same direction. If you blink, you'll miss the contest. The best doggers do their business in five seconds or less.

Roping cattle by the horns and hind feet has been a common method of doctoring and branding since the days of the open range. Team roping is a speeded-up version. The contest requires two cowboys, a header and a heeler. The header chases the steer and throws his loop around the animal's head, neck, or horns and veers off. When the rope is taut, the animal changes direction. The heeler follows behind and catches it by its two hind feet and jerks the loop tight before the steer steps out of it.

★ A dogger goes for the horns. (*Mark MacLeod*) ★

The heeler can't make his throw until the steer makes the corner.

Both men must dally, wrap their rope around the saddle horns, to take up slack and hold the steer. (Lots of team ropers have lost a thumb in a bad dally.) Time is called when both horses turn to face each other, with the steer in the middle, ropes taut.

The most popular roping steers are Corrientes, a Mexican breed with good-sized horns. Roping is hard on the horns. A hornless steer makes good ground beef but not a good target. That's why most rodeo steers wear horn protectors. With their special helmets strapped on, the steers bear a certain resemblance to World War II aviators.

A ROPER'S EXCUSES

Roping is one of the hardest and most essential cowboy skills. When a roper misses his mark, he has a truckload of reasons why. He can pin the blame on his horse, the steer, his rope, his luck. Here are some of the most common excuses heard around the rodeo arena:

The steer ducked.

The steer set up.

I was fighting my head.

I split the horn.

My horse checked out.

I caught the horse's foot.

I hooked my rope on a fence post.

I lost my concentration.

I blew my bubble.

My rope didn't feed.

I hit my slick spot.

The heeler missed the corner.

My horse stumbled.

My horse shut me out.

It was a new rope.

The chin strap broke.

Got a bad fly.

The steer jumped over my loop.

The barrier caught my rope.

RODEO ALL-STARS

★ Casey Tibbs, the Babe Ruth of Rodeo. (*PRCA*) ★

Every rodeo rider has his hero, the cowboy who inspired him to go give it the old cowboy try. Rodeo has two pantheons, the Pro Rodeo Cowboy Hall of Fame in Colorado Springs and the Rodeo Hall of Fame at the National Cowboy Hall of Fame in Oklahoma City. Both museums have enough gold and silver to look like a storage vault at Fort Knox.

The list of record holders include:

ALL-AROUND COWBOY: Larry Mahan (6 times) and Tom Ferguson (6)

SADDLEBRONC RIDING: Casey Tibbs (6)

BAREBACK RIDING: Joe Alexander (5) and Bruce Ford (5)

BULL RIDING: Don Gay (8)

CALF ROPING: Dean Oliver (8)

STEER WRESTLING: Homer Pettigrew (6)

TEAM ROPING: Jake Barnes and Clay O'Brien Cooper (5)

Cowboys have a special place in rodeo heaven for these cowboys, members of the gold buckle pantheon:

CASEY TIBBS (1929–90)

All-Around Champion
1951 and 1955

Casey Tibbs was the most widely known rodeo contestant that ever competed. Tibbs was a flashy dresser with a flair for showmanship. His trademark color was violet. Strong as a bull, but slight as a butterfly, Tibbs floated on a horse rather than anchoring himself to the saddle. His graceful technique worked: He was the saddle bronc champ six times in the 1950s. And he is the only champ to win both bronc events in the same year.

JIM SHOULDERS (1928–)

All-Around Champion
1949, 1956–59

Shoulders holds the record for the most championships—sixteen altogether. His gold buckle collection is large enough to circle his waist a couple of times. When he stopped riding broncs and bulls, Shoulders opened a rodeo school, produced rodeos, and raised rodeo stock. His bull Tornado was ridden only once in six seasons.

LARRY MAHAN (1943–)

All-Around Champion
1966–70, 1973

"Super Saddle," as he was known in the rodeo world, was a new breed of cowboy. Mahan was the first cowboy to qualify for the NFR in all three rough-stock events. More than any other cowboy, Mahan capitalized on his rodeo fame. His business ventures, including his own brand of western wear, have made him a wealthy man. Alluding to his business savvy, *Time* magazine once called him "the cowboy in the gray flannel suit."

RODEO COWGIRLS

ON THE PRO rodeo cowboy circuit, cowgirls are confined to barrel racing and vying for rodeo queen, cattle country's answer to prom queen. But that wasn't always the case.

At the turn of the century women began appearing as contestants in rodeos and such Wild West shows as Buffalo Bill's, Miller 101, and Pawnee Bill's. Prairie Rose Henderson, a Wyoming rancher's daughter, was the first woman to ride a saddle bronc—in 1901. About the same time, Little Annie Oakley dazzled the crowd with her sharpshooting at Buffalo Bill's. Roping and riding wasn't confined to men in pants. Trick rider Edith Tatlinger was the star cowgirl of the Miller 101. And world champion steer roper Lucille Muhall competed with, and frequently beat, the cowboys in early-day rodeo events. Little won-

der that aspiring cowgirls hoped to grow up and rope like Lucille.

During the depression cowgirl Tad Lucas earned more than $10,000 a year riding bucking broncs on the rodeo circuit. And she had plenty of competition. But after World War II when Rosie the Riveter went home, Connie the Cowgirl went back to the ranch. The rough stock was reserved for the men. Rodeo was big business and women were considered a sideshow. Probably for lack of bigger challenges, Dixie Reger Mosley, a cowgirl Evel Knievel, made a habit of jumping cars on her palomino.

A women's pro rodeo circuit still survives but it doesn't get the attention—or the money—it deserves. All-girl rodeos have six standard events: bull riding and bareback bronc riding (they're allowed to hang on with two hands), tie down and break-away calf roping, team roping, and barrel racing.

It's easy to admire a fast cowgirl on a faster horse. It's harder to understand what would possess a woman to ride a bull. That's the question Lynn "Jonnie" Jonckowski, one of the best on the women's circuit, has been asked for years.

> ★
> **Cowgirl Wisdom**
> The winners are always
> faster horses and
> younger women.
> ★

If they were complainers (which they're not), cowgirls would complain about the saddle gap, the rodeo version of the gender gap. Last year's bareback riding world champion cowgirl, Anne Stevens, won $2,666 at ten all-girl rodeos. Her male counterpart, Wayne Herman, earned

★ Early cowgirls had enough courage to fill their ten-gallon hats. (*Buffalo Bill Historical Center, Charles Belden Collection*) ★

★ Million-dollar cowgirl Charmayne Rodman races Scamper around yet another barrel. (*James Fain*) ★

$122,949 by competing in more than a hundred rodeos. Professional cowboys can support their families on their rodeo winnings. Most professional cowgirls see their winnings as "dress money" to help keep their family in spurs and boots.

The exception is barrel racing, one of the events on the program at a PRCA rodeo. Charmayne James Rodman, rodeo's Billie Jean King, was the first million-dollar cowgirl and only the third rodeo rider to attain that distinction. A nine-time world champion, she's the winningest rider ever in a single event. Last year Rodman won $110,868. She and her horse Scamper, a twelve-year-old bay gelding that used to work in her father's New Mexico feedlot, are crowd favorites.

Cowgirls mostly tend to barrel race, which rewards speed and agility. They race out of the gate and make a cloverleaf pattern around three oil barrels (or giant Coors cans), shooting dirt in their wake as they make their tight turns and then race for home. A five-second penalty is added for every barrel knocked down.

Barrel racing gives cowgirls a chance to show off their style as well as their horsemanship skills. The WPRA gives an award to the best-dressed barrel racer at the NFR. Sequins and spangles are de rigueur.

★ Bronc rider Tad Lucas smiled all the way to the hooter. (*Wyoming State Museum*) ★

COWBOY COURTSHIP

THERE'S SOMETHING ABOUT the way they walk. Something about the way they talk. Something about the way they dress. "I love the way cowboys look," admits one cowgirl, "despite the chew can in the back pocket and the slimy hat." Cowboy clothes can make any man look good, even tall, dark, and handsome. The shirt accents his broad shoulders, the trophy buckle keeps his waistline in check, the boots add a couple of inches, and the hats add a whole lot more. A good hat can prevent a gal from ever noticing a receding hairline or a bald spot on top. And a handlebar mustache can anchor his chin.

"I've always been attracted to cowboys," says one ranch wife. "It must be their charm and their sensitivity." Ranch women will tell you that their men are tough but tender. They have a special feeling for nature that borders on poetry when they try to put it into words. Every spring they see the baby animals and marvel at the miracle of life. When they come across a field of wildflowers, they'll stop and pick a bouquet. When they find a woman to love, they'll treat her like a queen. "Cowboys are romantics, extreme romantics, and ninety-nine out of a hundred of them are sentimental to the core," explained author Larry McMurtry, son of a West Texas ranch family. A cowboy will tell you that there's nothing more romantic than being around Mother Nature.

In the movies cowboys are always bonding with their horses. In reality there usually was a cowgirl back home. If not a cowgirl, she was a schoolteacher. In the early days of the range, teachers were the only fresh female faces around, and they were beset with suitors. Cowboys used to call women "calicos," in appreciation of their dresses.

★ It's true. Cowboys often do get married on horseback. (*Cattle Kate*) ★

(Cowboys still like women in dresses.) When punchers fell in love, they were said to have calico fever.

Many traditions have changed, but they've been replaced by new ones. Now when a cowboy is going steady, his girlfriend tears the Wrangler tag off his blue jeans. When a good old cowboy has had a little too much to drink on Saturday night, he might be brazen enough to try to bite the tag off the back of a good-looking girl's jeans.

Some girls are known as buckle chasers. They won't go out with a cowboy unless he's sporting a rodeo buckle. Some bold cowgirls custom-order their own belts. But instead of having their name carved on the back, they'll have their phone number engraved in leather. They'll also wear rattler

HOW TO KISS IN A COWBOY HAT

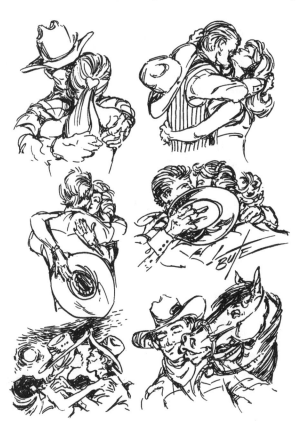

earrings—so you can hear them coming.

Country kids learn the facts of life at an early age. But instead of listening to the story of the birds and the bees, they learn about the bulls and the stallions. Many cowboys first learn about sex by sitting on the top rail and watching the stallions mount the mares. And cowgirls don't need Lamaze because they've coached dozens of cows and mares through the birth process. But there are some distinctions. Girls learn to turn their head when a bull mounts a cow. My cousin Kathy reminds me when she was sent home because of her gender. "They were breeding horses over at the Lewis ranch," she recalls. "We were all sitting on the corral watching them put the stallions in with the mares. All of a sudden my father turned to me and said, "You shouldn't be here."

Young cowboys are said to be as simple and direct as a stallion. But cowgirls will tell you that cowboys know how to move. They have lots of experience trying to match another being's rhythms. Riding a bucking horse often looks like some kind of wild sex act.

City boys may have a hard time finding a private place to neck. Cowboys, on the other hand, have no shortage of lovers' roosts: roll in the hayloft, sleep under the stars, bed down in the back of the truck (why else is the back of a truck called the "bed"). Ranch folks tend to avert their eyes and take the long way around when they come across a young couple in the throes of passion. Tolerant folks, they don't care where people make love as long as they don't do it in the corrals and frighten the horses.

Some cowboys never really ask their girls to be their brides. They let their actions speak louder than their words. One cowboy gave his girl a prize colt and a note saying that he was going to Nevada and would she like to go along. Before you could say "Powder River, let 'er buck," the wedding bells were ringing.

It's quite common for cowboys and cowgirls to get married on horseback. The bride and her horse have matching flowers in their manes and the groom has a hat on his head and a pint in his boot.

It's true that it's sometimes hard to choreograph the celebratory kiss. The cowboy hats sometimes get in the way. But after saying "I do," the bride and groom always ride off into the sunset.

Cowboy Wisdom

In a horse they call it loco, in a man they call it love.

A woman's heart is like a campfire. If you don't tend it, the flame goes out.

Never marry a woman with the kind of looks that you'd like to see on another man's wife.

A cowboy always chases a woman until she catches him.

HOW TO IMPRESS A COWGIRL

I know one cowboy who used to ride rodeo to attract the girls. He had his pickup line down pat: "Merle's my name, rodeo's my game." Here are a dozen more ways to impress a cowgirl:

1. *Ride a bull.*
2. *Stick to a rank bronc until the tooter.*
3. *Sport a trophy buckle.*
4. *Own a fast horse.*
5. *Let her ride your horse.*
6. *Drive a new rig.*
7. *Make your dog sit in back.*
8. *Buy a new hat.*
9. *Twirl her on the dance floor.*
10. *Get rid of your chew before kissing.*
11. *Offer to wear matching shirts.*
12. *Give her a Black Hills gold ring.*

★ A cowboy's first love is his girl. But a close second is his dog. (*John Morris*) ★

THE NAME GAME

Read down the roster of rodeo entries and you'll get a quick introduction to the cowboy name game. Steer wrestling champ Butch Myers has three children—Rope (1991 Rookie of the Year), Tie, and Cash. Not everyone has Myers's flair, but you won't find many—if any—Nicholases or Alexanders behind the chutes or in the corral. But you'll find dozens of guys with one-syllable names that only a guy can love: Ty, Tuff, Tee, Guy, Gip, Jake, Rex, Roy, Troy, Butch, Buck, Bud, Buster, Chuck, Clint, Kyle, and of course, Ote. Then there are the grown men whose childhood nickname kind of stuck: Rowdy, Rusty, Shorty, Cheater, Beaver, Mule, Kid, Slick, Smokey, Roach, Rooster, and Freckles.

Cowboy Wisdom

The four things a cowboy cherishes most are women and

horses and water and grass.

A married cowboy who comes home with a stray hair on

his collar better have a horse to match.

CHAPTER TWENTY-SIX

COWBOY MEDICINE

DOCTORING CATTLE IS part of a cowboy's job. He's as fast with a syringe as his grandfather was with a pistol. Old-timers had to shoot a cow to put her out of her misery. Cowboys today are expected to nurse the bovines back to health. Vets are reserved for special emergencies.

When cowboys ride through their herds, they're constantly on the lookout for signs of pink eye in heifers or foot rot in bulls, whose big hooves were not made for much walking. Sometimes their patrols are heartbreaking, as when they come across a couple of heifers that have gorged on green alfalfa and bloated or a calf that has frozen to death. Other times their discoveries are almost comical, like a calf that has poked its head through a rusty bucket or a cow that has stepped on a can and is now carrying it along.

Among their many skills, cowboys are midwives to cattle. Cows don't always give birth easily. When a cow is having trouble pushing, she's rounded up and brought to the barn to be pulled. The calf puller is a contraption that looks like a long pole with a hand crank on one end and two bars on the other. The bars are wedged against the cow's hind end and a chain or rope is wrapped around the calf's front feet. The cowboy slowly cranks the chain up and pulls the calf into the world. Pulling calves tends to give cowboys an inflated sense of their medical abilities. (More than one cowboy's child has been delivered at home. They even joke about it, as in "Johnny's wife calved out last night.")

There's an art and a science to calving heifers. Not everybody can tell that a first-time mother is going to spill before she actually spills. If the calf puller isn't handy, cowboys have to go it alone. I can remember my dad pulling off his coat, his sweater, and sometimes his shirt and thrusting his arm inside to get hold of the calf's feet to pull each time the mother cow pushed.

Cowboys give calves tender loving care. If a calf is sick and wet, the cowboy saddle-packs it back to the barn, while the mother cow follows behind. The pair are put in a stall in the barn for a couple of days until the calf is stronger. Sometimes a cowboy will come across a calf that is half frozen. This calls for stronger measures. He might take it home and warm it up in a bathtub full of hot water. Some ranch wives prefer to warm up a calf with an electric blanket or a hair dryer. (Hold the mousse.)

Cowboys, rather than vets, also take care of horses. They shoe them when necessary, treat wire cuts, deworm them, treat minor wounds. Every cowboy can tell war stories of soaking his lame horse's foot or floating his teeth when he

★ Winter rescue: Saddle-packing a calf home. (*Buffalo Bill Historical Center, Charles Belden Collection*) ★

couldn't eat (file any hooks or sharp points off grinding teeth). Unless the prize stallion is under the weather, it's unlikely that the vet will hear about the problem.

Their home remedies are enough to impress a rain forest witch doctor. Chewing tobacco is a ready relief for an insect bite or a minor cut. Vinegar cures hiccoughs. Baking soda helps indigestion, cinnamon relieves vomiting. And whiskey is good for anything. Not all cowboy remedies can be found in the kitchen. Bob Crosby, an old-time rodeo rider, once got gangrene from a tight cast. Doctors told him that they had to operate but he packed his bag and went home and resorted to an old ranch remedy. He wrapped his leg in an inner tube packed with cow manure. He swore that it saved his leg.

A cowboy's proven ability to cure ailments contributes to his general attitude toward medicine. He hates to call a doctor until the patient is practically at the pearly gates. They think it's a sign of weakness to dial a doc (and few ranches offer health insurance). Partly it's because a doctor visit takes all day, by the time you travel back and forth on two-lane highways and dirt roads. Sometimes

Cowboy Wisdom

Being a cowboy means

never saying it hurts.

Pain is just the other side

of feeling good.

He's too old to suck and

too young to die.

it's a necessity, as when the kids are sick and heavy snows have closed the roads. More basically, it's because the cowboy thinks he can doctor as well as the doctor. Why pay someone whose first question is "Where does it hurt?" (At least a vet doesn't have to ask.)

As a rule, cowboys treat themselves with less concern than they show their livestock. It probably comes from the fact that in the early days a well-trained horse was harder to come by than a hard-working cowboy and received better care. Cracked ribs or a broken finger can be tolerated. A man doesn't have to be able to walk to ride a horse. Even hemorrhoids, the curse of the cowpuncher, can be toughed out. If a cowboy consulted a doctor every time he got hurt, he'd have to move to town.

With rodeo cowboys, it's even worse. It's not uncommon to see a rodeo rider exploding from the chute with an arm in a cast or a knee in a brace; they don't let broken bones stop them. Bull riding champ Tuff Hedeman once rode a bull, waving a hand swollen to twice its normal size. "It ain't nothing but a hangnail," he scoffed. Rodeo cowboys accept injury and pain as part of their livelihood. The annals of rodeo are full of champs who rode while injured. Jim Shoulders, a rodeo legend who won sixteen world championships from 1949 to 1959, set the standard. At the Lewiston Rodeo in 1956, Shoulders was riding a bareback bronc that jerked his riding arm so badly that it broke his collarbone. Shoulders finished the ride and won first place. He came back the next day to ride two Brahman bulls and finish in the money.

There is only one exception to the rule that doctors and vets should be avoided at all costs: dogs. Cowboys don't think twice about taking their dogs to the vet. "They go in a heartbeat," says one ranch wife, whose husband has taken both of his dogs to the vet after they were stepped on by a horse. "The dogs came home with casts on their legs—one was green and one was pink."

Cowboy Wisdom

God heals and the doctor takes the fee.

One for a man; two for a horse.

RODEO WRECKS

★ A bronc rider bites the dust. (*James Fain*) ★

To outsiders, rodeo seems like a suicide game, especially the rough stock events. Consider the contestants: 150 pounds of wiry human muscle going *mano a toro* with a ton of snorting, pounding bull. There are groups that protest cruelty to animals in rodeo; but the animals most abused are the cowboys. Rodeo riders take their knocks—and then some. When 1992 world champion bareback rider Wayne Herman stepped up to receive his gold buckle in Las Vegas, he had a black eye, stitches above his cheekbone, and a sore elbow from being banged around in the chute when a bronc boiled over. Bob Henry, a steer wrestler, once competed with both arms in casts and tied for first place. Rodeo legend Jim Shoulders once broke his leg in five places. "You can't stop something like this from hurting," he said. "But you can damn well not let it bother you."

Top riders don't. By Labor Day every rodeo cowboy bears a sprain, a gash, bandaged ribs, or a combination of injuries. Many have been dragged semiconscious from one arena only to show up raring to go at the next. Rodeo cowboys have come to accept injury as part of their job. There's no injured reserve list. When a rodeo cowboy gets hurt, the paychecks stop. "If you're hurting you don't go home," said eight-time world champion bull rider Don Gay. "You just get in that car or plane and try to heal on the way to the next one."

Too often rodeo riders just tough it out. Their travels interfere with appointments with their family doctor, and even if they had time to see a doctor on the road, they wouldn't know whom to call. In 1982 Justin Boots came to their rescue. The bootmaker underwrote a mobile sport-medicine program that has eliminated some of the cru-elty to cowboys. "Before the Justin Program . . . you had to be feeling like you were practically staring at the undertaker before you'd resort to a doctor," said veteran bull fighter Ted Kimzey. Rodeo docs now follow the cowboys as they go down the road, seeing more than two thousand cowboys a year at more than fifty rodeos.

If rodeo had an injured reserve list, it would include bull riders who limp in with pulled groin muscles (the broad backs of bulls weren't designed for riding) and strained riding arms, not to mention what happens if they're on the ground and the bull sees red. Steer wrestlers often hurt their knees as they strike the ground jumping off horses going twenty-five to thirty-five miles an hour. They also are prone to shoulder injuries from rotating their arm to grasp the horn of a steer weighing three times their weight. Elbows, which absorb most of the shock, and knees, which have to awkwardly spur, are the Achilles heels of bareback riders. And bronc riders have knee problems from constant spurring and neck problems from their flying dismounts. An unlucky roper can leave a finger or two lying in the dust after a bad dally.

Here's an inside look at the most—and least—dangerous rodeo events:

Bull riders account for almost 37 percent of all injuries.

Bareback riders	23 percent
Saddle bronc riders	15 percent
Bull fighters	9 percent
Steer wrestlers	8 percent
Calf ropers	4 percent
Team ropers	1 percent

Cowboy Wisdom

One reason cowboys ride bulls is to meet nurses.

The easy events are dangerous. And the tough events

can be killers.

COWBOY'S ALMANAC

COWBOYING IS AN all-weather occupation. The postman gets all the credit, but the same and more can be said about cowboys. Cattle have to be fed, moved, and tended to, regardless of the weather.

Cowboys know firsthand the effects of searing drought, scorching sun, drenching rain, and freezing blizzards. Because they spend most of their lives outdoors, cowboys are weather junkies. When two cowboys meet, their first talk is of the weather. Old cowboy songs are full of tales of punchers suffering miserable dry spells or wet spells or both.

The last thing a cowboy does before he mounts up is check out the sky. Even in Arizona, a sum-

mer storm can appear out of nowhere, drench everything in sight, and then disappear. If an old hand sees a young kid in shirt sleeves, he'll quietly say, "By the look of them clouds, you'll need a good slicker."

Self-taught meteorologists, cowboys say that they can predict weather by observing various signs in nature. Animals are unusually restless before a rainstorm. And the hair on the necks of calves gets thick and shaggy in the months before a bad winter. A blizzard might be on its way when wildlife moves down from the hills and stays around day and night. Hard-edged clouds mean that strong winds are coming. One cowboy swears that he always brings along a heavy coat when the

★ Moving cattle to warmer pastures. (*Buffalo Bill Historical Center, Charles Belden Collection*) ★

clouds look like a horse's tail when it's running.

Rain is a special concern of cowboys and ranchers. But it's looked on with favor, not disappointment, so long as their slickers are handy and they're not in the middle of haying. "We need the rain," they explain. Most western states are hard up for moisture. A decade-long drought has dried up reservoirs, slowed rivers to a trickle, and turned grasslands into deserts. "The range is so dry the bushes follow the dogs around," complained one Nevada cowboy last summer.

Cowboys can tell when it's about to rain: when distant sounds are loud and sharp; when the wind is from the east; when leaves turn over and show their bottom sides.

Summer rains are often accompanied by incredible lightning storms. Keenly aware that

Cowboy Wisdom

The ground is bone dry when a single horse kicks up a trail of dust.

Sprinkles are for tenderfeet. Cowboys prefer downpours. They're good for the soul and great for the grass.

Winter fog would freeze a dog.

lightning will strike at the tallest thing around, a cowboy on horseback gets down off his horse and sits on the ground while the lightning is flashing. And he makes sure that he and his horse stay away from power lines or barbed wire fences. Bolts of lightning have been known to wipe out whole strings of cows huddled around wire fences.

When a cowboys says, "It's getting a little bit western out there," he means that the weather is building up to a near blizzard. Up north, wind and snow present special dangers. A norther can cause the temperature to plunge forty degrees in a few hours. When faced with a frigid gale wind, a cow does the only sensible thing she can think of and turns her rump to the wind. That helps solve one problem, but contributes to another—cattle start to drift in a bad wind, sometimes ending up hungry and tired miles from home. Before cowboys can take cover from the storm, they have to head the cattle to shelter. In the process, they often find weak calves that have to be saddle-packed back to the corral to keep from freezing on the open range.

It often snows when cowboys bring their cattle down from the hills. That's what happened to one ranch family in November. When I asked one of the cowboys what the weather would be like the next day, he replied, "Deep and still." What does that mean? "Deep as your ass and still snowing."

When asked how bad the winter was, painter Charles M. Russell sent back a small card that said it all. Showing a bony, starving cow surrounded by snow banks, the drawing was entitled "Waiting for Chinook." A chinook is a warm wind that melts the snow and lifts the spirits of cowboys in Montana and North Dakota. A chinook wind thaws the snow almost over night, allowing the cattle to get at the grass. Northern cowboys have a wise old saying, "If you don't like the weather, wait five minutes."

STORMY WEATHER

The ferocity of the weather out west matches the magnitude of the open spaces. As one old-timer put it, "Out here, the weather gets plumb wholesale." Because they spend so much time outside fighting against the elements, cowboys have a way with weather words. Here's a list of favorites:

Blue whistler	= a violent gale wind
Cayuse wind	= a cold east wind
Chinook	= a warm wind in the Northwest from the Japan current that melts the snow even in midwinter
Cow skinner	= a severe winter storm
Dust devil	= a whirling desert sandstorm
Duster	= a sandstorm
Fence lifter	= a very heavy rain
Goose drowner	= a cloudburst, heavy rain
Gully washer	= a hard rain
Hell wind	= a tornado
Idaho brainstorm	= a whirling sandstorm
Lay the dust	= a light sprinkle of rain
Norther	= a driving gale from the North
Oklahoma rain	= a dust storm
Pogonip	= Nevada's frozen winter mist
Sand auger	= a little whirlwind
Silver thaw	= a rain that freezes as it hits the ground
Squaw wind	= Washington's chinook

Cowboy Wisdom

Thunder does all the barking, but it's lightning that bites.

★

CHAPTER TWENTY-EIGHT

COWBOY GEOGRAPHY

COWBOYS HAVE TO navigate on the open range. One of the cook's jobs on early trail drives was to set the tongue of the wagon by the North Star and point the herd north. Huge ranches like the XIT would cross seven states moving their herds from winter to summer pasture. Before the drive began, the general manager would issue directions: "Keep your eye on the North Star and drive straight until you can wet your feet in the waters of the Yellowstone."

Even today, cowboys have an innate ability to find their way around. They take pride in being able to find cows that have holed up in a canyon or hidden themselves in the brush and have great disdain for dudes who get lost in the hills. "He couldn't find a cow if she was in his own bed" is how one cowboy described a tenderfoot.

It's an acquired skill, one learned after many miles in the saddle. Cowboys use common sense. They know that streams flow downhill. They make a point of remembering that the broken gate is near a bald hill or that the trail divided on a rocky ridge. "I've never been lost in the hills in my life," says one cowboy. "But I'd be lost in a city."

When a cowboy gives directions, he doesn't

talk about junctions and highways. He talks about arroyos and baldies and cedar brakes. Here's a cowboy's guide to geography:

Arroyo	a narrow gorge with steep dirt walls in the Southwest
Badlands	little vegetation, lots of erosion, mostly buttes and peaks
Baldy	a treeless mountain peak
Bench	a plain rising from a lowland
Bog hole	a mud hole that cattle enter smelling water and quickly get mired in
Bottom	low ground next to a river bed
Box canyon	a mountain gorge with one entrance and no exit
Breaks	rough land
Buckshot land	poor clay soil
Brush country	flat land with low trees and brush, as in Southwest Texas
Butte	a lone hill or rising over a lowland
Canyon	a deep valley with steep sides
Cedar brakes	broken land overgrown with scrub cedar
Coulee	a ravine or dry creek in the Northwest
Cross canyon	a canyon bisecting another canyon

Cut banks	a precipitous hillside or bank that drops off
Draw	a shallow natural drain for rainfall
Gully	a narrow ravine worn by running water
Gulch	a deep ravine or gully
Hogs back	a narrow ridge with steep sides
Mesa	a flat-topped hill
Range	open country where cattle graze
Slow country	a steep rocky trail
Wash	a gulch or a ravine

Cowboy Wisdom

Before you go into a canyon,

make sure you know how you're

going to get out.

GREAT COW TOWNS

The guidebooks are full of places to see traces of the Old West. Arizona has Old Tucson, Washington has Winthrop. But they're relics, not living and breathing cow towns. When cowboys head for town, they make tracks for Elko or Alpine or Miles City. And it's true that many are one-horse towns. Here are the best places to see signs of the New West.

ARIZONA

Sonoita
Prescott
Flagstaff
Seligman

CALIFORNIA

San Luis Obispo
Red Bluff
Salinas
Visalia
Caliente
Coalingua

COLORADO

Maybell
Grand Junction
LaPorte
Pueblo
Greeley
Durango

IDAHO

Caldwell
Nephi
Garden Valley
Pocatello
DuBois

MONTANA

Miles City
Dillon
Red Lodge
Wisdom
Ovando

NEVADA

Elko
Reno
Winnemucca

NEW MEXICO

Clayton
Grady
Cimarron
Jal

NORTH DAKOTA

Dickinson
Zap
Medora
Sentinel Butte
Watford City

OKLAHOMA

Blanchard
Checotah
Henryetta
Grove

OREGON

Burns
Pendleton

SOUTH DAKOTA

Bellefouche
Rapid City
Mobridge

TEXAS

Lubbock
Burkburnett
Guthrie
Alpine
San Angelo

UTAH

Ogden
Vernal
Spanish Fork

WYOMING

Cheyenne
Cody
Kaycee
Douglass
Laramie
Riverton

BARDS IN BOOTS

THERE'S SOMETHING ABOUT the life of the cowboy that brings out the poet in a man. Maybe it's the campfire. Maybe it's the sunsets. Always, it's a sense of place. Cowboy poetry celebrates the history, traditions, and everyday life on the ranch. A deep love for the land and the fear of losing his chosen lifestyle have inspired many a cowboy to put down his reins and take out a pencil—and write a "pome."

The results tell tales of the everyday life of cowboys, from bucking broncs and cagey cows to Stetson hats and stove-up punchers and anything else that can be stuffed into rhymed couplets. Shakespeare in boots they're not. Like any horse, the rhyme sometimes bucks and the meter shies. But the energy and emotion lets the reader hear the voices of the cowboys and see the land that they love. The poems have even more power when recited by people who live what they write.

Baxter Black started out as a vet before he turned to verse. With three books, a syndicated column, and hundreds of performances under his belt, Black is one of the best-known bards. In one of his poems, he dreams about team roping with the legendary Leo "the Lion" Camarillo.

Buck Ramsey is a stove-up Texas cowboy, put in a wheelchair by a big bronc and a busted cinch. With more time on his hands, he braids rawhide and writes poetry poignant enough to make a grown cowboy cry.

Wally McRae, is a fifth-generation Montanan. His cattle graze on ranges next to one of the country's largest strip mining operations. With wit and

★ On the open range, the campfire was like the corner bar: a place for swapping stories, singing songs, and reciting poems. (*Buffalo Bill Historical Center, Charles Belden Collection*) ★

wisdom, his poems emphasize his ties to the land and his cowboy values.

Waddie Mitchell, a buckaroo bard with an inimitable handlebar moustache, used to be a ranch foreman. He hasn't sold his saddle, but he has sold books, tapes, and videotapes. When not on the poetry circuit, Mitchell calls Elko home.

Bronc rider Paul Zarzyski (rhymes with bar whiskey) has a master's in literature. The free-verse rodeo poems in his *Rough Stock Sonnets* rock and roll, twist and shout.

The cowboy's fondness for verse has spawned poetry magazines that feature everything from recipes for son-of-a-gun stew to ads for bull semen. They include: *Dry Crik Review* (P.O. Box 51,

Lemon Cove, CA 93244), *BOOTS* magazine (P.O. Box 766, Challis, ID 83226), *American Cowboy Poet* magazine (P.O. Box 326, Eagle, ID 83616), and *Cowboy* magazine (P.O. Box 126, La Veta, CO 81055).

For a taste of cowboy poetry, old or new, try one of the anthologies edited by Hal Cannon and published by Gibbs Smith. Or track down one of the many cowboy poetry gatherings. At least once a month somewhere in the West cowboys are meeting to pour out their hearts in their poems. There are more than fifty a year, from Alberta, Canada, to Alpine, Texas. Most cowboys read their own work, others recite from the canon of early-day cowpunchers. (Many in the audience know the old poems by heart.)

Cowboy Wisdom

Reciting poetry is like a haircut. If it's good, you feel like a million bucks. If it's bad, you hide your head under a hat.

★

JANUARY

Elko Cowboy Poetry Gathering
Western Folklife Center
P.O. Box 888
501 Railroad St.
Elko, NV 89801
(702-738-7508)

Colorado Cowboy Poetry Gathering
Arvada Center for the Arts and Humanities
6901 Wadsworth Blvd.
Arvada, CO 80003
(303-431-3080)

MARCH

Texas Cowboy Poetry Gathering
P.O. Box 395
Alpine, TX 79831
(915-837-8191)

National Festival of the West
Box 12966
Scottsdale, AZ 85267-2966
(602-996-4387)

APRIL

Visalia Spring Roundup
35664 Rd. 112
Visalia, CA 93291
(209-627-0287)

Grand Junction Cowboy Poetry Gathering
Museum of Western Colorado
Box 20000-5020
Grand Junction, CO 81502-5020
(303-434-9814) or (303-243-7711)

Oklahoma Cowboy Poetry Gathering
National Cowboy Hall of Fame
Oklahoma City, OK
(405-478-2250)

MAY

Cowboy Symposium & Celebration
Ranching Heritage Association
Box 43201
Lubbock, TX 79409
(806-742-2498)

JUNE

Alberta Cowboy Gathering
Box 2392
Pincher Creek, Alberta
TOK 1W0 Canada
(403-627-4733)

Cannonball Cowboy Poetry Gathering
P.O. Box 536
Mariposa, CA 95338
(209-742-6064)

JULY

South Dakota Cowboy Poetry and Music
   Roundup
300 Sixty St.
Rapid City, SD 57701
(605-394-4120)

New Mexico Poets' Gathering
Silver City Museum
312 W. Broadwy.
Silver City, NM 88061
(505-538-5921)

Cowboy Poetry and Music Jamboree
Steamboat Springs Ski & Resort Corp.
2205 Mt. Werner Cir.
Steamboat Springs, CO 80487
(303-879-6111, ext. 470)

AUGUST

Great Pikes Peak Cowboy Poetry Gathering
5550 N. Union Blvd.
P.O. Box 1579
Colorado Springs, CO 80901
(719-531-6333)

Montana Cowboy Poetry Gathering
P.O. Box 818
Lewistown, MT 58457
(406-538-5436)

Arizona Cowboy Poetry Gathering
Sharlot Hall Museum
415 W. Gurley St.
Prescott, AZ 86301
(602-445-3122)

SEPTEMBER

O'Keefe Ranch Cowboy Festival
Box 955
Vernon, BC VIT 6M8
Canada
(604-542-3168)

Curly Fletcher Cowboy Poetry and Music
    Festival
High Horse Productions
475 Church St.
Bishop, CA 93514
(619-873-8405) or (619-872-1596)

Idaho Cowboy Poetry Gathering
Caldwell, ID
(208-888-9838)

OCTOBER

Lincoln County Cowboy Symposium
Museum of the Horse
P.O. Box 40
Ruidoso Downs, NM 88346
(505-378-4142)

Red Steagall Cowboy Gathering and Western
    Swing Festival
Texas Agricultural Extension Service
500 Jones St.
Fort Worth, TX 76102-5484
(817-884-1945)

Wyoming Cowboy Poetry Roundup
Central Wyoming College
2660 Peck Ave.
Riverton, WY 82501
(307-856-7184)

Durango Cowboy Poetry Gathering
P.O. Box 2571
Durango, CO 81302
(303-259-1388)

NOVEMBER

Western Poetry Writers Party and Reading
    Celebration
Moab, UT
(801-259-7814)

DECEMBER

Rodeo Cowboy Poetry Gathering
    (Held in Las Vegas during NFR)
Western Folklife Center
P.O. Box 888
Elko, NV 89801
(702-738-7508)

OH, GIVE ME A SONG

COUNTRY WESTERN MUSIC has always been long on country and short on western. Probably that's because Nashville happens to be east of the Mississippi. Most cowboys in Nashville are the rhinestone variety.

How can you tell a country singer from a cowboy singer? It's not easy. Both are fond of hats and boots. They both sing with a drawl. But if you listen to the words, you can spot the cowboy every time.

Country singers are far from their country roots. Many of their songs are about the three D's: drinking, divorce, and depression. Cowboy singers, on the other hand, stay close to the land they love. Their lyrics tell tales of the three R's: riding, roping, and rodeo. Instead of singing about the mock heroism of truck drivers, they celebrate the quiet courage of early-day trail drivers.

Cowboys have always loved music. Early cowboys sang songs around the campfire, serenaded themselves and the cattle at night, and kicked up their heels when they reached the end of the trail. If they didn't have an instrument (they usually didn't), they clapped their hands. When it comes to music, not that much has changed. A cowboy's radio is always on, he croons old melodies in the saddle, and he still loves to dance.

Classic cowboy songs tell stories, rich in detail, of the cowboy's daily work and life.

Unschooled musician-songwriters set their verses to traditional English, Irish, and Scottish folk music. "The Cowboy's Dream" is sung to the music of "My Bonnie Lies Over the Ocean." Like all folk music, the cowboy songs had multiple versions, reflecting regional differences and personal idiosyncrasies. The classic song, "The Old Chisholm Trail," had enough verses to be sung from San Antonio to Abilene without repeating a stanza.

Old cowboy songs take several forms: slow songs sung to the pace

★ Chris LeDoux sings songs of the rodeo world he left behind. (*Ira Mark Gosten*) ★

of a horse's gait like "I Ride Old Paint," and toe-tapping, bronc-riding songs like "The Strawberry Roan." The cowboy's serious side is reflected in songs like the "Cowboy's Lament" (better known as "The Streets of Laredo"), about a young cowboy "wrapped in white linen and cold as the clay," or the equally haunting "Little Joe the Wrangler," whose life ended under the hooves of stampeding cattle. Modern performers, such as Don Edwards, the Texas Troubadour, can make a grown cowboy break down and cry with his heartfelt renditions.

Cowboys also sang upbeat trail-herding tunes like "Whoopi Ti Yi Yo"; practical jokes like the "The Zebra Dun," an outlaw horse; and bawdy songs like "The Whorehouse Bells Were Singing." No cowboy singer was complete without a morning holler and a cattle call or two. Harry Jackson and Peter LaFarge were two of the saddle masters. Their recordings are available from Smithsonian/Folkways Productions.

When Hollywood put a hat on a guitar player

and called him a singing cowboy, it took him far from his roots. Early cowboy songs were written for harmonicas, fiddles, and mandolins, instruments that could be packed in a saddlebag. Expensive and large, guitars were left behind at the ranch. During the 1930s and 1940s, as cowboys ventured away from the classics, they learned to play guitar, and they learned how to yodel. Gene Autry, Roy Rogers, and the Sons of the Pioneers made the public aware of cowboy music but didn't do much for cowboys.

To be a cowboy singer today, you have to have a musical voice and a cowboy soul. That could be said about Red Steagall, Don Edwards, and Michael Martin Murphey, the evangelist of western music. Murphey is responsible for convincing Warner records to put out a new label, Warner Western, that features all three, along with the

Cowboy Wisdom

Songs sound better

when sung around the

campfire.

If you can't sing—dance.

★

Real cowboys don't

line dance.

Cowboys dance every

dance as long as their

bladders and feet

hold out.

★

Sons of the San Joaquin, a California trio.

Today cowboy singers are exploring their roots and reinventing cowboy music. Chris LeDoux traded his bronc rigging for a guitar and writes songs about rodeo. George Strait team ropes when he's not making music. But the hands-down favorite of most cowboys is Ian Tyson, a folk singer turned rancher turned cowboy singer. Tyson writes songs about cutting horse competitions in Fort Worth, saddlemakers from Colorado, riding fence at the timberline.

The son of a working cowboy, Tyson worked ranches in Alberta and rode the rodeo circuit in his teens and early twenties. When a rodeo accident cut short his athletic career, he moved to Toronto and teamed up with Sylvia Fricker to form the popular folk duo, Ian & Sylvia. Immensely popular in Canada in the 1970s, Tyson gave up the bright lights of the big city and moved back to Alberta to work on a friend's ranch, as presaged in his song "Four Strong Winds." In the early 1980s, with a ranch of his own in Alberta that should have kept him busy, Tyson embarked on a second musical career. His first recording of cowboy songs, "Old Corrals and Sagebrush," included traditional cowboy classics like "Windy Bill" and "Colorado Trail," as well as songs of his own. Since then Tyson has recorded four more "cowboy culture" albums, mostly his own compositions. Songs like "Springtime in Alberta," "Since the Rain," and "Cowboys Don't Cry" are destined to become classics. They're available on Stony Plain Records.

To keep up with the renaissance in cowboy music, aficionados subscribe to the quarterly *Song of the West*. For information contact 136 Pearl Street, Fort Collins, CO 80521 (303-484-3209).

DANCIN' AND PRANCIN'—
"COWBOY STYLE"

COWBOY DANCES CAN BE COMPLICATED AND VARY
ACCORDING TO AREA AND INDIVIDUAL — DANCE LESSONS
FOR BASICS ARE A GOOD IDEA —

① RIGHT HEEL

② BACK

③ RIGHT HEEL

④ BACK

⑤ LEFT HEEL

⑥ BACK

⑦ RIGHT TOE

⑧ BACK

⑨ LEFT HEEL

⑩ BACK

⑪ RIGHT STOMP

HERE ARE THE STEPS
TO A TRADITIONAL COWBOY
DANCE CALLED THE
"16 STEP" —

PARTNERS TURN
HOLDING FINGERTIPS

REPEAT

⑯ SHUFFLE AGAIN

⑮ SHUFFLE

⑭ GIRL TURN

⑬ MAN TURN

⑫ RIGHT STOMP AGAIN

BUTE

MAKING MUSIC

Cowboy singers haven't made the hit parade—yet. But if cowboy musicians like Michael Martin Murphey have their way, lots of folks will hear and appreciate the cowboy songs that their ancestors loved. Murphey, a cowboy-music evangelist, is the man behind the Warner Western record label and the WestFest music celebrations. All over the West cowboys and cognoscenti gather to celebrate western music, old and new. Often dressed in Tom Mix hats, Texas boots, Montana chaps, gauntlets and gloves, the cowboy performers put on shows that weave together music and song, poetry and storytelling. They're fast becoming the 1990s version of the Wild West shows. Here are some of the favorites:

APRIL

Cowboy Songs and Range Ballads
Buffalo Bill Historical Center
P.O. Box 1000
Cody, WY 82414
(307-587-4771, ext. 248)

JUNE

Cowboy Music Gathering
Western Folklife Center
P.O. Box 888
Elko, NV 89803
(800-748-4466) or (702-738-7508)

WestFest
Red River, NM
Littlehorn Communications
2132 N. Andover Ct.
Oklahoma City, OK 73120
(405-755-8288)

AUGUST

WestFest
Reno, NV
Littlehorn Communications
2132 N. Andover Ct.
Oklahoma City, OK 73120
(405-755-8288)

SEPTEMBER

WestFest
Copper Mountain, CO
Littlehorn Communications
2132 N. Andover Ct.
Oklahoma City, OK 73120
(405-755-8288)

NOVEMBER

Western Music Festival
Western Music Association
P.O. Box 64852
Tucson, AZ 85740
(602-323-3311)

DUDE RANCHES

THE DUDE RANCH tradition is almost as old as the cattle ranch. Right from the start, some ranchers discovered that taking in paying guests in the summertime was one way to keep the cash flow moving. Howard Eaton and his three brothers started the first dude ranch in 1884 when they built cabins for dudes right on their ranch near Medora, North Dakota. They later moved to Wolf, Wyoming, and specialized in rehabilitating city boys gone bad.

Basically there are two kinds of dude ranches: guest ranches and working ranches. Guest ranches cater to city folks who want a taste of the West with all the amenities: a hot tub on every porch. Guest ranches cater to total greenhorns. They're taught to bridle and saddle their own horse, if they want. But usually they're treated like pampered guests; dudes can spend their days in the saddle or decide to go hiking, fishing, or swimming.

Working ranches, on the other hand, offer pay-to-work vacations. They allow guests to participate in whatever's going on—roundup, branding, cattle drives. Because these ranches are rooting-tooting cattle ranches, there are fewer guests, simpler lodging, and lower prices. If you need a telephone or television in your cabin, this is not the place for you.

★ Winter feeding at the Home Ranch. (*L. Kendrick Jones, Joe Sage*) ★

SADDLING UP

Guest ranches offer daily trail rides as well as hot tubs and hiking. Working ranches offer something more: a chance to step into a cowboy's boots and participate in the daily life of the ranch. Depending on the time of year, that means rounding up strays, sorting and gathering cattle, branding calves, trailing cattle to and from summer pasture, shipping cattle, herding horses, and packing salt to the high country. Being a guest, of course, you have the choice of doing as little or as much as you want.

Spring roundups and fall cattle drives are two of the best times on a ranch. What's the difference? On a roundup, where you'll gather the cattle, you'll stay on the home range, close to the house. On cattle drives, on the other hand, you'll trail cattle from one range to another.

Cattle drives are not for everyone, especially for dudes who have never sat a horse. They're often hot and dusty or cold and wet. Days are spent in the saddle, evenings are spent around the campfire, and nights are spent on the ground—under the stars. As a new rider, you'll probably ride flank or drag, beside or behind the herd. But the scenery is bound to be great and you'll learn a closely guarded secret: Trail drives really do start with a loud "Yee haw," cow talk for "Let's go."

If you want to visit the West, try a guest ranch or ranch resort. If you want to live the ranching life and know what being saddlesore really means, a working ranch is for you. Guests get a taste of the cowboy lifestyle as they trail cattle, round up horses, brand calves (the old-fashioned way), and spend a night on the trail. They also have plenty of time to enjoy the abundance of wildlife—elk, deer, and wild horses—that make their home on the range.

Knowing how to ride is a must. In fact, some working ranches won't take inexperienced riders or children under twelve. A few ranches allow guests to work with horses being trained or help cut cattle. And if you're really good, the cowboys may teach you

★ Getting a leg up is always the hardest part. (*Julie Chase*) ★

how to rope. Here's a list of working ranches where any cowpuncher would be happy to park his saddle:

ARIZONA

Grapevine Canyon Ranch
  P.O. Box 302, Pearce, AZ 85625
    (602-826-3185)

Price Canyon Ranch
  P.O. Box 1065, Douglas, AZ 85607
    (602-558-2383)

CALIFORNIA

Hunewill Circle H Ranch
  Summer: P.O. Box 368, Bridgeport,
    CA 93517 (619-932-7710)
  Winter: 200 Hunewill Rd., Wellington,
    NV 89444 (702-465-2325)

Quarter Circle U Rankin Ranch
  P.O. Box 36, Caliente, CA 93518
    (805-867-2511)

Spanish Springs Ranch
  1102 Second St., San Rafael, CA 94901
  (800-228-0279 [in-state]) or (800-228-8262
    [out of state])

COLORADO

Aspen Canyon Ranch
  13206 Country Rd., Star Rte., Parshall,
    CO 80468
  (303-725-3518 [ranch]) or (812-473-8747
    [office])

Everett Ranch
  10615 Country Rd., Salida, CO 81201
    (719-539-4097)

MONTANA

Circle Bar Ranch
  Utica, MT 59452 (406-423-5454)

Hargrave Ranch
  Thompson River Valley, Marion, MT 59925
    (406-858-2284)

Sweet Grass Ranch
  Melville Rte., Box 173, Big Timber,
    MT 59011 (406-537-4477 [summer]) or
    (406-537-4497 [winter])

NEVADA

Cottonwood Ranch
O'Neil Basin, Wells, NV 89835
(702-752-3604) or (916-832-4861)

SOUTH DAKOTA

Western Dakota Ranch Vacations
HCR 1 Box 9, Wall, SD 57790 (605-279-2198)

UTAH

Preston Nutter Ranch
P.O. Box 221, Price, UT 8501 (801-637-0947)

WYOMING

David Ranch
Box 5, Daniel, WY 83115 (307-859-8228)

High Island Ranch
Box 71, Hamilton Dome, WY 82427
(307-867-2374)

Lozies Box R Ranch
Box 100, Cora, WY 82925 (307-367-2291)

Shively Ranch
1062 Rd. 15, Lovell, WY (307-548-6688
[winter]) or (406-259-8866 [summer])

TX Ranch
Box 453, Lovell, WY 82431 (406-484-2583)

*Some of the more popular guest ranches
are:*

C Lazy U Ranch
Box 879, Granby, CO 80446 (303-887-3344)

The Home Ranch
Box 822, Clark, CO 80428 (303-879-1780)

Lost Valley Ranch
Rte. 2, Sedalia, CO 80135 (303-647-2311) or
(303-647-2495)

Lone Mountain Lodge
Box 69, Big Sky, MT 59716 (406-995-4644)

Mountain Sky Guest Ranch
Box 1128, Bozeman, MT 59715
(800-548-3392) or (406-587-1244)

Y.O. Ranch
Mountain Home, TX 78058 (512-640-3222)

HOW TO BE A GOOD DUDE

First off, don't feel bad about being called a dude. You've got great company. Teddy Roosevelt started out in the West as a dude—a four-eyed weakling. But after three years ranching in Dakota Territory, where he rode on roundups, broke broncos, trailed cattle, and served as a deputy sheriff, Roosevelt had earned his spurs. He was so inspired by cowboys that he organized a cowboy cavalry—the Rough Riders.

Naturally, cowboys are very gender conscious. Female dudes used to be called dudeens or dudettes. Today they're more likely to be called lady dudes.

Dude or dudeen, you should follow the ranch rules if you want to earn your spurs. They include things such as:

Don't argue with the wrangler.
Listen and learn.
Stay on the trail.
Don't gallop past horses moving at a slower gait.
Respect nature.
Don't criticize the cook.

★ The bull should have the last word. (*Montana State Historical Society*) ★

About the Author

Michele Morris, a fourth-generation Montanan, grew up on the family cattle ranch. She spent twelve years in New York as a magazine editor and writer before returning home to write *The Cowboy Life*. She is married and is the mother of two sons. She divides her time between New York City and Montana.